How to Succeed With NLP

Go from Good to Great at Work

Anne Watson

CAPSTONE

This edition first published 2010
© 2010 Anne Watson

Registered office
Capstone Publishing Ltd. (A Wiley Company), The Atrium, Southern Gate, Chichester, West
Sussex, PO19 8SQ, United Kingdom

For details of our global editorial offices, for customer services and for information about
how to apply for permission to reuse the copyright material in this book please see our
website at www.wiley.com.

The right of the author to be identified as the author of this work has been asserted in
accordance with the Copyright, Designs and Patents Act 1988.

All rights reserved. No part of this publication may be reproduced, stored in a retrieval
system, or transmitted, in any form or by any means, electronic, mechanical,
photocopying, recording or otherwise, except as permitted by the UK Copyright, Designs
and Patents Act 1988, without the prior permission of the publisher.

Wiley also publishes its books in a variety of electronic formats. Some content that
appears in print may not be available in electronic books.

Designations used by companies to distinguish their products are often claimed as
trademarks. All brand names and product names used in this book are trade names,
service marks, trademarks or registered trademarks of their respective owners. The
publisher is not associated with any product or vendor mentioned in this book. This
publication is designed to provide accurate and authoritative information in regard to the
subject matter covered. It is sold on the understanding that the publisher is not engaged
in rendering professional services. If professional advice or other expert assistance is
required, the services of a competent professional should be sought.

Library of Congress Cataloguing-in-Publication Data

9781907293054

A catalogue record for this book is available from the British Library.

Set in 11 on 14 pt Calibri by Toppan Best-set Premedia Limited

Printed by TJ International Ltd.

Dedicated to my brother, James Watson, Managing Partner of Watson Woodhouse, not only good but great.

Contents

Introduction

Success on our own terms would seem to be what we are all pursuing; the only question being what success actually means for you. Once you know what you want then you are already well on the way to achieving that success. You can then start to work out what small or large steps you need to take to get there.

No matter how good you are, you can always be better. This book will show you ways of working out what success means to you and then will help you to identify clear steps you need to take to get there. If you measure success in terms of personal development, promotion, tangible achievements, recognition, salary increases or other benefits, the way to win all of this is by adding and creating value in the job you are doing.

How do you move from being good at work to being great? How would you like to become the greatest thing that ever happened to your boss and to your company? As soon as you become this prized asset then all the rewards that you hold to be important will follow on.

Practical advice that works is the theme for this book. Get ready for tips and techniques that will first of all help you define what success is to you and then the kind of effective examples that will help you as you move along the path from good to great.

This book will highlight common situations, dilemmas, challenges and problems in work and life and suggest different Neuro Linguistic Programming (NLP) based solutions that will give you just what you need to transform yourself. We will find out more about NLP in Chapter 1. But this is not a handbook to NLP; it is all about your success and ways to improve performance at work so that you are reenergized, in control and giving a sparkling performance in everything you do. All you need to know about the NLP techniques is that they will work.

The starting point here is to realize that successful people who are leaders in their field tend to be 100 % responsible for their own lives. What happens to them, what they achieve and where they are in life is underpinned by a fundamental belief that everything lies in their own hands and no one else's. These people do not have chips on their shoulders about their upbringing, their education or the hand that life has dealt them. They take what they have and through their own attitude and behaviour they create what they want.

Like twenty-three-year old Russian Alina Ibragimova, one of the world's best violinists. Having been beset by wracked nerves prior to every concert and every performance, one day when she was twelve she decided that she would never be nervous again. And she wasn't. How would you like to know some fast, simple and effective techniques to eradicate the possible barriers to your success? Would you like to know some ways to gain that level of control over what happens to you and over your emotions? How can you make sure that your response to life's events is the one that you want rather than the one you find yourself with?

Achieving what you want is something that needs to be worked at. Simply doing one thing right isn't enough to get to the next level. If you want to be successful at work you have to do a good job, be seen to be doing that good job, forge brilliant relationships with colleagues, customers and suppliers and you need to be sure that you are seen in the right light for the kind of promotion or reward you are looking for.

Personal relationships are important in work as well as in our personal lives, and if you want to pursue a life's dream, then you need to be aware of the invisible and the unspoken.

Recognizing who you are and how you function is an essential starting point, and then you move on to understanding others. How do you get what you want out of your communication with others? How do you say what you mean, and make sure you understand what others are saying to you? How do you gain that flexibility and sharpness of focus that will mean you stop fighting shadows and instead bring into sharp relief the real issues that you need to address.

Reading this book will provide you with new and effective tools and techniques that will help improve your working relationships, make a positive impact on your career and deliver the ability to take control of your life, your communication, career and success. What is it that you want to improve in your working life? Do you want to earn more, get that next promotion, win a place on a prized development programme, be valued or just want a feeling of satisfaction that you are needed? All of this lies in your hands and your control; it is just a case of knowing how to do it.

There's never a better time to leave the negative behind. Miserable thoughts, depressed attitudes, bad news and mutual moaning are addictive, corrosive and highly infectious. Let's make the starting point a positive one, as once you change your mind-set to one that is constantly looking out for the good points rather than the bad, you will suddenly find it more energizing and uplifting than complaining could ever be.

In an age where the ability to control your work life has spiralled out of control because of external events, the world of work has never been more challenging and changing. Traditionally, careers used to follow steady paths and relatively predictable routes. If you worked hard and stayed loyal to your employer, then stability and pay rises would follow. Of course, some businesses don't make the grade and people lose their jobs through no fault of their own but generally there seemed to be a natural law of cause and effect. The rules of engagement used to be that working hard would create a long career, culminating in the award of a pension. Those rules have changed so your behaviour has to change to match them.

The twenty-first century has seen a shift in attitudes by both employers and employees. Since the '90s, an eclectic career has increasingly come to be seen as acceptable and to have advantages. Businesses are changing and adapting more quickly than ever at all levels; in their structure and in the way they operate to deliver profitable results. A person who has spent their entire career with one company may be considered to be lacking in breadth as a company changes.

By the same token, individuals today can choose where they want to work and choose to leave if they don't like it. People who are seeking to achieve talk about quality of life and a good work life balance and will make tough decisions to leave a company if it is not satisfying at every level. However, this choice might seem to be restricted in difficult economic times, with the tightening of the credit market and the sudden and unrelenting pace of 'downsizing' or 'rightsizing'. Surely this must mean your choice is being limited by external circumstances and your ability to control what is happening is diminished? This book will show you that this is not the case, and that by taking responsibility for what happens to you, the opposite can happen. You will have control of your life and your career. In order to do this, you need the skills to take charge of your own destiny and the tools and strategies to use in the workplace to achieve success.

Change, choice and control lie ahead; you can learn the tools you need to go from being good to being great in the workplace. It all lies in your hands and will be achieved through your efforts alone – with the help of the chapters ahead.

Your Route to Success with NLP Signposts

Setting the scene

Think about that moment when you wake up in the morning. Do you bounce out of bed with enthusiasm or do you eventually crawl out yawning? A reluctance to get up is not just physical tiredness, it is mental tiredness as well. People who love life and who look forward to their day are glad to get up. If life is not like that for you, then decide now that you will regain the high levels of motivation and career hunger that bring satisfaction at all levels. This is the time to manage your own motivation and to fire up the passion for personal success and reward. It is easy to slip into comfortable ways in a job and not be aware of time slipping past. Are you sure that every day brings with it something new and an opportunity to test yourself in different ways? Falling into ways that are routine and predictable is not the route to take if you want to make yourself stand out and grow a satisfying career. Great people are enthusiastic and energetic, seeking out their own motivation. If it does not naturally come your way at the moment, then use the ideas and techniques in this book to find new life and vitality in the skills that you bring to your job and the energy you bring to your team. Now is the time to aim higher, do more, give more and ultimately get more.

Statistics show that one person in five goes to work and does an outstanding job. The rest do either a good job, an average job or a below average one. Success will come if you put yourself in that top 20% of highly effective people and, better still, influence people around you or in your team to give more of themselves to the job. Then tangible differences will be made, businesses will thrive and you will be acknowledged. People who are eager and ambitious need to have a stockpile of behavioural tools and techniques that they have mastered. These will help facilitate meaningful change and personal advancement. Successful people are purposeful and they know that flexibility is the key to success. Now is the time to focus on what you want out of life and what you are prepared to change to achieve it.

What do you *really* need to do to be successful? How do you set your goals, achieve these results, overcome obstacles along the way and have the influence over your work that you need to? How can you have more influence over other people and make sure that your negotiations lead to success? To enjoy your career, create harmonious and productive relationships in the workplace and progress with commensurate financial reward, you will need to be confident that you are making the right impact and developing the level of self mastery required to be effective. This way you will be sure that you are behaving in a way that brings you the response you are looking for. The result of that is that you will live the life that you want.

What can I do for my employer?

Today, most people will be doing more work in the same hours and for the same pay or, worse, for a pay cut, and with no bonuses. Long-term views of careers may be hard to find as it is well nigh impossible to know what is going on behind the closed doors of the board room.

For you, what does this mean? How can you be sure that you are appreciated and your contribution is acknowledged? How can you improve your performance and develop your skills when it would seem that budgets have been cut and there is no money available for the kind of training and development programme that you would ideally like to follow? Perhaps there is a feeling that life is not under your control but under that of the employers. How do you use all of your skills to do the best you can and to make sure you are valued?

The starting point of thinking will be to recognize that the only way to live is by accepting that you are in control of your own life, so it is all down to you. Although we cannot choose the circumstances in which we are born and brought up and although we don't know what can happen to us along the way, we can alter how we react to them. Control lies in how you respond to life. Look at the successful people in your organization who seem to be valued and appreciated.

They are no different from you and no more capable than you. However, it is highly likely that they probably have more self belief, more motivation and they will actively seek out opportunities to improve their fortunes. Look at these people hard because they are your role models and you will soon be adopting and improving on their techniques that have taken them to the top of their field.

If you also decide to start thinking about 'What can I do for my employer' rather than 'What can my employer do for me?' you will have made two major shifts in attitude that will already reap extraordinary results. Show your employer how good you are and your employer will want to support you in all the ways that will add to your success.

Becoming a prized asset

More than this, how do you make sure that you are the most prized asset that your employer has got? How do you make yourself indispensable and make sure that you are seen in a different and positive light? When you shift your personal performance from good to great, you will be able to command the next stage of your career and be that rare commodity an organization is looking for – a brilliant contributor. Reliance on an employer to be the person who controls the development of your career is a thing of the past. There is now a mutual responsibility and it is not just academic qualifications that make a rounded and valued employee. Make sure your boss appreciates you and you will then be in a better bargaining position for moulding your role to suit your growing skill-set.

Alex Mitchell, Head of Influencer Relations at the Institute of Directors, believes firmly that you are 100% in control of your success. A particular passion of his is to ensure that young school leavers and graduates find their way into jobs that will allow them to develop their talents to the full. He advocates a path into the workplace via meaningful volunteering where skills such as project management, leadership, budgeting, self-discipline and team playing can all be learnt. These are tangible, practical skills that can be added to any academic qualifications, thus increasing chances at interview and in the job market. Structured skills based volunteering is a way to give back to the community while gaining useful skills.

The next vital piece for Alex is ensuring that business leaders pay close attention to this experience won in a different yet valid environment. Alex's vocabulary is made of the words that you want to hear – inspirational, challenging, positivity, realism, curiosity. His message is clear – career opportunities may not seem to be around but there are always opportunities to create them for yourself.

What is NLP?

Neuro Linguistic Programming is considered by some to be a science of excellence, a means of establishing excellence and then modelling it. Originally developed and promoted in the 1970s by its founders, John Grinder, a linguist, and Dr Richard Bandler, a gestalt therapist and mathematician, it is an effective and rapid way of addressing problems people have in terms of confidence, communication and phobias. They were greatly influenced by the work of Milton Erickson, a renowned psychiatrist who specialized in medical hypnosis. By modelling his way of addressing the unconscious mind through hypnotic language patterns Bandler and Grinder went on to develop NLP as techniques that can be taught to improve personal effectiveness.

The prime focus of this book is learning how to develop the life skills needed to create the life that you want by utilising all of these NLP tools and techniques to the full.

Let's start with what are called the 'Presuppositions of Neuro Linguistic Programming'. These are the core beliefs that summarize what NLP is all about, giving the framework within which these tools and techniques have been developed. I will be using these presuppositions throughout the book as signposts. Each one will be explored to see what it means for you and how you can address it to add to your skills in your job.

The presuppositions used are as follows. They will be explained further as we come to each one through the book:

♦ **Everything in NLP should increase choice.**
♦ **There is no failure, only feedback.**
♦ **People have all the resources they need to succeed.**
♦ **If what you are doing is not working, try something different.**
♦ **The mind and the body form a linked system.**
♦ **The map is not the territory.**
♦ **We are always communicating and the meaning of the communication is the response you receive.**
♦ **We are all in charge of our minds and therefore our results – the law of cause and effect.**

♦ **The person with the greatest flexibility controls the system and will have the greatest influence. There are no resistant people. There are just inflexible communicators.**
♦ **Behind every behaviour there is a positive intention.**
♦ **People are not their behaviours. Accept the person and change the behaviour.**

NLP links language and neurological pathways to a pattern of behavioural techniques that result in the brain being reprogrammed in order to do things more effectively and therefore achieve goals. This means that NLP shows you how to think differently, act differently and get the results that you choose. Add to this the vital application of how this can add zest to your job and increase the control that you have over it and the success you aspire to. Suddenly you can experience the exhilarating feeling that choice lies with you. I will be taking a different presupposition of NLP to guide every chapter and linking it to the desired attributes of successful people.

NLP and you

NLP is not for the intellectually idle. Focus, concentration and consistency will mean that by taking committed short steps and by using tried and tested techniques, behaviour will change and if behaviour changes, then so does everything else. The definition of madness is continuing to do the same thing over and over and expecting a different result. This is the NLP lucid and clear path to the sanity that change brings with it. You may well be using some of these techniques unconsciously already, so you will be adding to your portfolio of NLP skills. Whatever we call them and whatever they are, the important point is that they work.

The need for clear communication is not restricted to the workplace. Personal relationships depend on you being able to express clearly what you think, what you feel and what you want. What matters in communication is not what you think you are saying but what meaning someone derives from what you have said. Have you ever sent out an e-mail and been taken aback by the tone or content of the response? This is probably because the words you used did not convey the meaning you intended. Add to this the fact that words form only part of communication, in addition to body language and other signs, and you can see that getting it right in the office environment is a path fraught with potential pitfalls.

Change – the route to success

In the course of my work in head hunting and executive coaching, I often find that people want to know how to change and how to get better results. Self-knowledge is a great thing and it is important to know how to use that personal mastery to bring about change where you need it. Self-knowledge needs to be followed by effective action.

'The person with the greatest flexibility controls the system.'

What does this mean? That the person who is prepared to change is the one who will be more likely to be in control of relationships. By change I mean change of style, change of perspective, change of language, change of mindset, change of tone and general subtle changes of approach.

This book, therefore, will bring you ideas on how to tackle issues that before have seemed impossible. In the course of the book you will work towards a strategy for your personal plan for individual success and you will define the milestones along the way. Small steps are always the best way to work towards a goal so decide now that in the next month you will utilize and practise the techniques that you need to help you get to where you need to be. Fortune favours the brave and those people who are brave, who are prepared to open up their minds sufficiently to embrace new techniques and methods of developing are those who will reap greater rewards. We are not looking at personal survival. We are seeking personal satisfaction and gratification in a career with the inevitable positive impact that it will have on life at home.

Setting your goals

What exactly do you want to achieve? Rather than working your way through the book and taking in the information as you go along, decide now what your goal is. What is so important to you that you are ready to go through a process of change to get it? Are you aiming for major transformation, a moment of enlightenment about your career? Are you going to use it to enable you to achieve your next promotion within a twelve-month time span? Will you be reading it with the objective of raising your profile at work so that you will be appointed Project Manager? Could it be that you just want to lift yourself above the 'redundancy zone' and be happy to stay in a job?

The way to achieve the best results is to have a clearly articulated goal. When you set off in the car or on train, heading off for a destination, you usually know where you want to end up.

You might not have every detail of the route mapped out but you do know where you want to be when the journey ends. In career terms you need to have that clarity about what you want and nothing will divert you from this bigger picture.

Once you have set a serious goal, you can then set the milestones for getting there. Make sure that the formulation of your goal is positive and that it is moving you towards what you aspire to, rather than shifting away from something that you don't want, that you feel negatively about or something that you fear. If you don't know where you are going, how will you know when you get there? If you just keep following the path, you may wake up one day aged fifty and realize that you are not doing what you wanted and time has slipped by.

Look at your work life and think about what you can do to move from good to great, to be recognized as a high performing person and to have the recognition and satisfaction that will go with it.

Here are a few thoughts about what you might be considering:

♦ further training and development;
♦ more responsibility;
♦ better relationship with your boss;
♦ better working relationships with colleagues;
♦ promotion;
♦ a team to manage;
♦ a change of product portfolio;
♦ international experience;
♦ relocation;

◆ a new job;
◆ greater confidence;
◆ more empowerment to make decisions;
◆ greater influence;
◆ being listened to;
◆ more money;
◆ an opportunity to shine.

In the course of this book we will be looking at what can help you along the road from good to great and we will also be examining what could be holding you back. Sometimes limiting beliefs about what you can do and what you are capable of are born from past experiences that simply do not apply to the person you are today. These can stand in the way of achieving goals or even having the confidence to articulate an ambitious goal. Your upbringing, your family, your education and your personal experiences can help as well as hinder. You can now look forward to expunging limiting beliefs from your life and having added momentum in the pursuit of your goal.

Ways to formulate a powerful and compelling goal

The SMART technique is a recognized way of helping clarify your thoughts about what you want. Here is the way to think through what you are looking to achieve:

Specific. A goal needs to be specific rather than general and you need to be able to answer the following six questions:

Who is involved?
What do I want to accomplish?
Where is it?
What is the time frame?
What do I need to do and what are the constraints?
What will I get when I accomplish the goal?

Measurable. These are the milestones you will be able to set in place to help you towards your goal so that you know you are on track, hitting your target dates and maintaining the energy you need in order to get there. You will ask yourself questions such as 'How much?' 'How many?' 'How will I know when it is accomplished?'

Attainable. As you work through the process of identifying the goals that are most important to you, you will begin to see the ways you can make them happen. You will identify the attitudes, abilities, skills, and confidence that you have that will allow you to reach them. You will grow in your abilities to reach the goals you have set so that they become more attainable as each day passes. You will identify missed opportunities in the past and this time you will be able to do everything in your power to get there.

Realistic. The goal can be high as well as realistic. Make it something you are willing and able to work towards. Only you know how much you are prepared to give in order to get there. Be sure that every goal represents substantial progress and that you have the motivational force to get there. If you believe you can do it, then the goal is realistic.

Timely. Be sure to give your goal a time frame. This is what will give it a sense of urgency and will give it the energy it needs to get there. If you decide that your goal is 'I will be promoted to General Manager and get a salary hike to go with it', then you need also to anchor it in a time frame. A goal that you will unconsciously be working towards is one that says 'Within twelve months I will be promoted to General Manager and I will have a 10% salary increase and an improved comparison.'

Let's move now from the theory to the specific and formulate a goal that is important and specific for you:

1. **Make it positive.** Now that you have decided what your goal might be, make sure that you state the goal positively. This is the sure way to convert it into reality. For example, you might want to say: 'I want to create a career that has new challenges and opportunities for personal growth.' This would work rather than 'I don't want to be doing the same old thing next year and feel I haven't moved on.'
2. **Give it context.** Be sure to put it in the right environment where you can see and hear where it will take place. This gives it more power and energy.
3. **Make it yours.** Be sure that this is a goal that is fulfilled by you. For example, a goal that will succeed is one where you say: 'I want to win sponsorship from my company to qualify as an accountant.' Saying 'I want my boss to sponsor my accountancy exams' is now outside your control and unlikely to succeed.
4. **Examine the consequences.** Think through the changes that success in achieving this goal will bring with them and be sure that this is what you want. Have you thought through the impact on you personally, your family, your way of life and your friends and family?

5. **Make sure it is worthwhile.** Remember that you will be putting energy into achieving this goal so make sure it is absolutely what you want and that is something that will enhance your life at a number of levels.

Using all of those guidelines to help you work through what your goals are, fill in this chart to help you formulate your thoughts:

WHAT I WANT TO ACHIEVE AT WORK

In 1 month	In 3 months	In 6 months	In 1 year	In 2 years

Thinking about your goals will have brought with it a sense of reality about the level of changes you will need to make in order to get there. As you work your way through this book you will find numerous ways to help you. You may even find that you want to do more than you currently think you can. These NLP techniques will give you a sense of certainty and confidence. Now is the time to raise the bar of your personal success and to get the kind of career that will bring with it the fulfillment you are seeking.

Take the time now to close your eyes and visualize the time when you have achieved the goal you have written down. Think of where you will be sitting and what will have happened around you that is different. For example, if you have decided that you are going to be promoted, see yourself sitting in the appropriate office. Look in your desk drawer and look at your new business cards that reflect the change in title. Put them back and look around you and hear the buzz of your team at work. This is your future and you have created it. Take the time to absorb the feeling of this success and create a clear memory. Now open your eyes with the determination to get what you want.

Write down your goals somewhere as a constant reminder of your big picture goal – on a screensaver on your computer, or a note in your desk diary on the Monday of every week. Little notes that you can put inside a book, a briefcase or a desk drawer are the little surprises that will spring out at you and remind you of where you are going. People put photographs on their desk of their families, reminding them of why they are working. Why don't you put the photo of the car you will buy, the holiday you will go on or the house you will live in? Find some kind of tangible symbol of what your goal is and place it somewhere that will remind you of what you are doing. Whatever it is, make it ever present today so it becomes the norm in the timescales you allowed yourself.

Right – let's press on! A compelling future awaits.

2

What Does It Take to Get What You Want?

"Everything in NLP should increase choice"

Greater choice in everything you do will open up greater vistas and broaden horizons. Suddenly you will be doing what you want rather than what you seem to have been given. Variety and choice lie ahead!

So who is the ideal employee?

Part of my role as a head hunter is to write job descriptions and job briefs. A key part of this is the section in the job brief entitled 'The Ideal Candidate'. This is where I work with my client to define the qualifications and the experience that will be required of this paragon of virtue that we are seeking. I will be defining the kind of academic qualifications, technical experience and industry knowledge that is vital for success. More importantly, I will be listing the kind of personal qualities that the employer will be looking for. This ideal person is likely to be energetic, a great team player, a good communicator, positive, decisive, confident, a good networker and someone who is full of curiosity. What are the chances that I am going to be looking for people who are negative, difficult to get on with and with low self esteem? Zero. No one wants to bring people into a business who are going to be difficult to manage and tough to assimilate into the team.

A national newspaper interviewed the Managing Director of a leading PR business who declared with pride that they never employed people who had a 'couldn't be bothered attitude'. Funnily enough, I doubt if many people ever have. Another client is adamant that they will only recruit if the candidate proves to be exceptional. Surely this is what we should all be looking for everywhere we go? For businesses to thrive, they need to be bringing in people who have talent and who have the attitude and mindset to add value to the organization. In order to be one of those people, in addition to developing your skills in whatever discipline you have chosen, whether it is finance, marketing, sales, purchasing, PR, Human Resources, IT, medicine, education, physiotherapy – whatever skills you develop technically and academically, you need to match them with personal strength so that you improve your success and your influence in the organization.

Have you got what it takes?

Do you think you have got the qualities it takes to be the successful employee, the person who is relied on to perform well and who is destined for a star studded career? When your boss is reflecting on the team, are you the person who will spring first to mind as the one who is indispensable? Do this simple test and start thinking about what you have got that an employer is looking for. By exploring just where you think you sit on this scale of good to great, you will identify attributes that you will want to focus on. You will then find that each of the next chapters takes each attribute in turn and develops the ways in which you can increase your skills and control the course of your career and success. Use this as a starting point for measuring where you are now and then growing your ability to change how you do things and improve your results.

The Attributes and Qualities of the Successful Employee: The Questionnaire

Instructions

Look at the list of words below and decide how appealing you find them. Then grade them on the rating of A, B, C or D to reflect the degree to which you agree with them. Put the letter in the relevant box and move to the next question.

For example, if the word you have to look at is 'Party', use your immediate reaction, that is to say the feeling, the behaviour, the reaction or the instinct that it arouses, to decide where you stand.

Don't think too hard about it but give your instant reaction. Play along, do it light heartedly and quickly and see how you get on. You can either do it in this book now or you can go to www.annewatson.co.uk and do it online to get an instant and tailor-made report sent back to you.

A = Spot on! It's what I am and what I do
B = Getting warm. It's a lot like me, a lot of the time
C = Not quite me but no violent reaction against it. I am not holding my hands up in horror
D = No way! This just isn't me

		A	B	C	D
1	Win				
2	Alive				
3	Hesitate				
4	Result				
5	Consistent				
6	Alone				
7	Connect				
8	Engage				
9	Voyage				
10	Alarm				
11	Restful				
12	Options				
13	Reward				
14	Determined				
15	Solitary				
16	Many				
17	Withdraw				
18	Imagine				

		A	B	C	D
19	Eager				
20	Active				
21	Wait				
22	Assured				
23	Variety				
24	Team				
25	Private				
26	Discussion				
27	Disinterest				
28	Downside				
29	Quiet				
30	Plan				
31	Perhaps				
32	Tried and tested				
33	Individual				
34	Space				
35	Reflection				
36	Explore				
37	Potential				
38	Routine				
39	Deadline				
40	Try				
41	Experiment				
42	Collaborate				
43	Inward				
44	Chatty				
45	Detect				
46	Danger				
47	Vibrant				
48	Organize				
49	Worry				
50	Spontaneous				
51	Combine				
52	Sociable				
53	Reserved				
54	Known				

Now you have finished, transfer your scores into the score grid below. The numbers in the grid correspond to the question number from the test above. Take the answers you have given and allocate yourself points in accordance with:

A = 4; B = 3; C = 2; D = 1

For example, if you have answered D to question 32, write 1 in box 32. When you have completed the grid, add the numbers up across horizontal lines and enter the total in the box provided. Thus, questions 1, 10, 19, 28, 37 and 46 should be added together, and so on.

1	10	19	28	37	46	Total Positive
4	13	22	31	40	49	Total Confident
2	11	20	29	38	47	Total Energetic
9	18	27	36	45	54	Total Curious
8	17	26	35	44	53	Total Communicator
3	12	21	30	39	48	Total Decision maker
5	14	23	32	41	50	Total Flexible
6	15	24	33	42	51	Total Team player
7	16	25	34	43	52	Total Networker

As the grid above shows, the nine attributes and qualities of the successful employee are:

1. Positive attitude (Chapter 4)
2. Confident (Chapter 5)
3. Energetic (Chapter 6)
4. Curious (Chapter 7)
5. Communicator (Chapter 8)
6. Decision maker (Chapter 9)
7. Flexible (Chapter 10)
8. Team player (Chapter 11)
9. Networker (Chapter 12)

Positive Attitude

20–24 You have a natural optimism and the ability to bounce back which means that you radiate a strong belief that things will work and you will inspire those around you. Be careful to check your facts so that this positive attitude has its roots in reality and that it is aligned to your goals.

12–19 Is it nature or nurture that has given you an occasional reluctance to build your hopes up? If you are bracing yourself for disappointment, you may be in danger of creating your own reality. How much of the time do you sit on the fence? Sometimes a healthy scepticism will be a way of pulling the wild optimists back and making them reflect. Sometimes it could throw a bit of a damper on the team.

1–11 Are you protecting yourself against potential failure? Perhaps you have had your hopes dashed before so you are now careful not to get your hopes up and not to concentrate on what might be. You dwell on harsh reality with no gloss and no spin. Life is tough and you're primed to see trouble ahead. If the world is a dangerous place for you, perhaps you may not derive the enjoyment and pleasure from work that you could. What is holding you back?

Confident

20–24 You have a breezy self assurance that is transmitted to others and will mean that others look to you for a lead. You know what you are good at and you are ready to step forward with opinions, views and ideas. As a result you may be more prepared to take risks than others as you know what you are good at and what you can do. Align this confidence to underlying capability and crystal clear goals and you will be a force to be reckoned with in the business.

12–19 You are generally quite confident but you allow yourself moments of self-doubt and questioning. This will mean that your colleagues will know that when you commit to doing something, you are as sure as you can be that you can do it. You are, therefore, likely to be more approachable than your more confident colleagues as people know that you are prepared to reconsider your views and decisions. You know you are right most of the time but now and again you waver and you reconsider.

1–11 You currently seem to have low levels of self assurance which may be a momentary thing caused by whatever is going on in your life at the moment. As a result you find it hard to be sure that you are doing the right thing, revisit decisions you have made and worry a lot, which could have an impact on your health and well being. Is this uncertainty holding you back?

Energetic

20–24 You are someone with high levels of energy that you bring to your job. Either you are in the office bright and early or you stay later in the evening, always something to do and ready to dash around and do it. You have an external focus and you love the buzz of a busy environment and you contribute toward it. Using your energy to achieve your goals will enhance everything you are working for.

12–19 When you are feeling full of energy, you know how to get on and do it. Sometimes you may have a problem motivating yourself and you can lose the momentum of the situation. What would happen if you experienced high levels of energy all of the time instead of now and again?

1–11 Are you feeling at a bit of low ebb, finding things a bit of an effort? Life may seem a bit challenging at the moment and you are working hard to find the resolve and the energy to deliver all that you need to. What do you need to do differently to regain the sparkle in your life?

Curious

20–24 You love finding out new things. You wonder what is round the next corner and a sense of what you don't yet know. You delight in finding out new facts, new information and you are driven by the thrill of uncovering new possibilities. New, different and unexplored are words that set you buzzing. For you, the joy is in the journey rather than arriving at the destination.

12–19 In a sense you enjoy the place where you are and while you are interested in the new and the different, you are content with what you know. When you are given the right stimulus, you will be willing to explore. In order not to get entrenched in the familiar, you might want to start looking around and see what you might be missing.

1–11 An appealing life for you is one that gives you the security of the known and the familiar. Perhaps there is a danger that you could go down predictable tracks. The down side of this is that not only do you not have any awareness of what you might be missing, you may be seen by others to be disinterested or disengaged. Perhaps you are engrossed in your own world and not ready to get involved with others?

Communicator

20–24 You know how to put your message across. You like to get engaged with people across a number of media and you like to stay in touch. You will know how to use e-mail, telephone contact and face to face meetings to the best advantage. You are an initiator and someone who makes things happen. People will look to you to get things going and to be the organizer.

12–19 You are reasonably comfortable in speaking, writing and getting the message across. When it matters you are there and you make the necessary contact. You may not always see the need to write, e-mail or call and there may be occasions when you miss an opportunity to get in touch. You know how to communicate and you do it often enough for your own needs. What would happen if you did it a little more often?

1–11 You are happy in your own world of thoughts and ideas. You are not disinterested in others, you just do not always see the point in calling writing or getting in touch. As a result, people may miss the valuable input that you can give. Your ideas may be overlooked as you don't necessarily volunteer them and others don't know that they should be asking for them. Do you think you could benefit from exchanging thoughts and ideas with others?

Decision maker

20–24 You are clear about what you want and you know how to make your mind up. You like life to be clear and you are happy when you are organized and working to a definite deadline. Making a decision may bring you a sense of relief that you have closed off those other options so you can focus on the goal you have established.

12–19 There are matters on which you are clear and you know what to do and how you want to do it. Sometimes, however, you may hesitate and deliberate before you make the decision. This may be necessary reflection that leads to better decision making. It may also be undue procrastination. What applies to you and how does it affect your work life?

1–11 You may find it quite hard to make a decision. Could it be perhaps that you are not clear about your goals? Maybe you are lacking in confidence or unsure what it is that you want? This 'haziness' can mean that you may hesitate over a decision and people around you may be waiting for you to make the next step. Do you want to be a decision maker or are you OK with other people stepping up, meaning that you follow on behind?

Flexible

20–24 You love new challenges and you like to see variety and rethinking in many aspects of your life. The new and the untested hold great attractions for you. As a result you look positively at new projects, and you are always feel ready to take on challenges you have not faced before.

12–19 You like to have change in your life if you can see that there is a point. You don't do change for change's sake although you have an open mind. You have a solid reference base of the tried and the tested and you use it to help you move forward. New things are interesting for you rather than essential. If asked to take on something new, your likely response will be a positive one.

1–11 You have a certain reluctance to move away from the warmth and comfort of what is familiar and known to you. You like to know where you are and to have done it before. New tasks or projects at work could alarm you and you may be nervous about trying something if you haven't done it before. You may not like risk taking and prefer to stick with what you know you can do and what you can control. What do you fear from change?

Team Player

20–24 You love being part of a team and you probably have always been involved with a group in one way or another, whether it is football, rugby, netball or cricket. You see the benefits of working with others and you actively seek out others to work with. You enjoy the exchange of views and the debate that goes on in a team. Working independently may feel slightly uncomfortable to you as you need the energy of the team around you for you to work at your best.

12–19 You are happy to be part of a team and if you are asked to work with a group you will be pleased to be included. You are equally pleased to be working on your own so if you have to spend one or two days a week working from home, you will find it a welcome change of working environment.

1–11 You probably see yourself as a self-sufficient and resourceful person who can think things through and manage independently. You probably have a lot of strength of character and you are not prone to disclosing information to all and sundry. You like to work by yourself and you will thrive when working in an office with the door closed. Have you tried pooling your resources with your colleagues and see what team work can do?

Networker

20–24 Forging connections with people will come easily to you. You like to chat, to meet new people and to keep up with them. Facebook was made for people like you. You engage with the world and you are interested in others and what they are doing. You will have a long list of people that you know and you will enjoy adding to their number. What more can you do to make that network work for you and for them?

12–19 You see the value in having contacts and connections and you probably have a certain group of people that you stay in touch with and who you value. However, you are not keenly motivated to add to the number so you will take opportunities to meet people as they crop up rather than actively hunting them down. People are important to you but you don't need to keep adding to their number.

1–11 You probably have a small number of valued friendships as you don't believe that large numbers necessarily equate to quality. You are more likely to be introduced than to introduce and you will not have making people connections at the top of your agenda. In the workplace you may not know everyone around and as a result, maybe everyone won't know you. Have you thought what you might be missing out on by maintaining such a low profile?

Remember that this isn't something cast in stone – it is a gateway to stimulate thinking about what an employer wants and what you seem to have and how you want to behave. The successful employee also needs to deliver on their potential and on their promises, not just talk about them. Also remember that these are just some of the qualities you need in order to be successful. There are other things you will bring to work that will be valued and needed.

Next steps

A high octane performance in the workplace relies on skilful command of these attributes. They will smooth the path to success and they will bring about that shift from being good at what you do to being great. Continuing to do things the same way and expecting a different result is a definition of madness. The truly successful person does not have expectations that events will merely unfold and success will happen. Success, as you will see in the course of this book, is what you create for yourself through your own actions and your mindset. It is what you do for yourself and what you do for others. The real secret of success is defining what you want out of life and then, having established those goals, accepting that you are 100% responsible for getting there.

Look now at your results and see what it is that you seem to be good at. Consider the areas where you may wish to work and develop more. You will form an idea of where you want to concentrate, using the tools and techniques that you will find as we go through the stages in this book. Each attribute will be taken in turn and explored in a separate chapter. Before you read each chapter, look at your score and think how you may wish to improve on it and where you will concentrate. The route from good to great requires effort and this book will show you simple and effective exercises that will help you get there. Change lies in your hands and the person who is the most versatile and ready to embrace new ways of working and behaving is the one who will excel and reap the rewards you are looking for.

The scale of good to great

Before you move on to the next chapters that will unlock the tools, tips and techniques that will allow you to develop the skills you need to be a superb performer with life at your feet, look at the grid and mark on it your current score. Then write in bigger, bolder figures where you would like to be on that scale. If you are already a 9, go off the scale. Outperforming expectation is a wonderful goal in itself.

	1 GOOD	2	3	4	5	6	7	8	9 GREAT!
Positive									
Confident									
Energetic									
Curious									
Communicator									
Decision maker									
Flexible									
Team player									
Networker									

Now is the time for you to move up the scale of greatness and to use the tools and techniques to get there.

3

How to Learn From Experience

"There is no failure, only feedback"

Moving towards feedback, recognizing the value of every-thing that happens, even when it is a different result from the one you may have imagined

In order to go from good to great, you must have the humility to accept feedback – the candid views and opinions of others and something you might perceive to be criticism. The best kind of team member is the person who provides reasoned and constructive criticism. Just as you don't want people to praise you for work that is in fact below par, you don't want to be giving insincere praise. The way to help others improve is to tell them what they are doing well and where they can improve. Don't be a people pleaser, be a people improver. Annual appraisal systems are the opportunity to review what has gone well throughout the year and what could have gone better. Play your part in creating a climate of mutual supportive feedback and everyone's performance will improve in incremental leaps.

There is no failure – only feedback. This is one of the presuppositions of NLP and indeed is something that is accepted at all levels in all organizations, starting in primary schools and never finishing. It means that life is a process of continuous learning and it is possible to learn from every situation. We learn from history, we learn from reflection on life's events, actions and behaviour. We learn from the viewpoints of others and the people who learn most and learn fastest are those who invite the opinions of others, particularly people whose experience is greater than yours and whose input you value. It is good to know what went well and what could have gone better. However, it requires a certain resilience to listen and accept the opinions and views of others.

In the course of my headhunting work I met Chris, who was promoted from an internal sales support role to an external Business Development role. He loved the new challenges that this brought with it and he got on well. A new Sales Director, Neil, was appointed who accompanied Chris on most of his customer meetings. At first, Chris was nervous and slightly resentful of what he perceived to be potential interference until he realized the power of Neil's style. When they left every customer meeting, Neil gave Chris direct and specific feedback on his performance, telling him what he had done well and what he could have improved on. He did not hold back on any of the detail. When he had finished, he then asked Chris to comment on how he had performed in front of the customer and suddenly Chris found himself giving feedback to his boss. Chris learnt that humility and a constant desire to improve makes everyone resilient in the face of feedback.

It stands to reason, therefore, that if we are going to progress from good to great, we need to be actively seeking feedback from peers, colleagues, the boss, customers, anyone you interact with. It also means that if you are going to be valued as a colleague in the organization, you need to be someone who is helping others to grow. This can be achieved partly through being prepared to give robust and meaningful feedback. How do you do that without bruising the feelings of friends and damaging their self esteem? Help is at hand – the feedback sandwich!

The Feedback Sandwich

Imagine a situation where you want to point out something that is not working in someone else's behaviour or work output. Let's say you have to point out to a colleague that a piece of work they have done is unsatisfactory. A direct approach may well work – 'the proposal you sent me is full of gaps and inaccuracies. I can't possibly send that out so please re-do it.' The more robust and confident person will take that in their stride. However, most people will feel deflated, crushed, demotivated, upset or unappreciated to one degree or another. What might be meant as an objective criticism of work may be interpreted as a personal criticism.

Out and about in my headhunting role, I met John, the General Manager of a manufacturing plant in the Midlands. In the face of changing markets, his job role expanded and he needed to liaise closely with the sales team. He had no wish to work with sales as he saw them as the perpetrators of the trouble the business was facing. He moved their offices into a different building and did everything he could not to engage with them. He was regularly told by his boss and by colleagues that what he was doing was wrong, not in the best interests of the business and that his actions were dividing what should be a united business. The feedback was formal in meetings with his boss, informal in chats with colleagues and even more informal with friends in a pub. John's response was to defend his position, insisted that he was right and that the proposed collaboration was a waste of time. He blocked all of this negative feedback and within six months he was fired.

How can we reconstruct a more effective feedback model that would deliver the message in an efficient but less punishing way? The best way would be to create a 'feedback sandwich', something that works like this:

A   Set a positive context by choosing to praise something that is good in terms of the piece of work, the behaviour or performance.
B   Focus on what is wrong.
C   Set the scene with how it will be put right.

How might this work in reality?

A   I appreciate the time you have dedicated to doing the pre-meeting work for our team building event. Your commitment and support to the team is something that will help us achieve our goals and I know that you are seen by others as a key team member.

B   Two of the three questionnaires that you did online were filled in incorrectly so could not be scored, thus preventing us from gathering all of the data that we need for the session tomorrow.

C   I know that you will deal with this immediately as you will want to ensure that the team programme runs smoothly.

Learning to handle negative feedback

It is always easier to accept praise than it is to deal with negative feedback. Remember the dreaded school reports and how it always seemed that parents focused on what had gone badly rather than on what had gone well? The likelihood in life is that what stands out is what is done badly. Decide now that your response to this will be one that welcomes the opportunity to do things better.

In order to take the defensiveness out of your reaction to unsettling feedback, use curiosity as a way to receive this news in a positive way. You could say, 'How do you suggest I change this?' 'How might you have handled it differently?' 'What can I do next time to improve?'

A key response is to thank people for criticism. This is disarming and it is honest. 'Thank you for your comments.' If you think they are wrong, start with the positive and begin with:

'I appreciate what you are saying and I wondered if perhaps there might be another way of looking at this.'

Indirect feedback

Useful feedback is not always spoken or written down. Sometimes it is there but not immediately apparent and it has to be looked for. The way to find it is be tuned in, to have heightened awareness of what you see, hear or what you notice in terms of dynamics. Subtle messages can be sent to you by colleagues and you are just not seeing them. These scenarios could be colleagues sharing cups of coffee but not including you. There could be meetings that are taking place that you never seem able to attend. E-mails may be going around that don't have you on the distribution list. Maybe your e-mail relationship with others is not as vigorous as it might be and you just haven't noticed. Pay closer attention to what is happening. Focus on the frequency of your e-mails with colleagues and notice the language. Are they short and to the point or do they acknowledge you as a person?

Take time to look around and listen. What is happening in your immediate circle that represents feedback on how you are perceived? When people are saying the right words such as 'Let's get on and do it' or 'That won't be a problem', perhaps their body language is at odds with their language. Be on the alert for any mismatches that could be signaling that you have a problem.

The starting point of meaningful change is being receptive to the views of others and you will be much more receptive to their feedback if you make steps towards appreciating their difference.

Understanding the difference of others

Remember the frustration of doing business with people who don't seem to be able to explain what they want? Your preferred way of taking in information may be one that needs facts, information, data, spreadsheets, dates and times. You may be dealing with someone who just doesn't give you what you need, talking about theories, ideas, plans while what you need in order to get to the heart of the matter is to put plans in place. Businesses thrive on processes and systems that then allow strategic thinkers the structure and the latitude to get things done and to grow new ways of working. Have you ever been in a situation when your boss is telling you to plan a meeting, plan a conference, order stock, implement a project yet does not give you sufficient information to do it properly? Either you have to go ahead anyway and run the risk of getting it wrong or you have to irritate them by pinning them down on the nitty gritty detail. There are a number of ways through precise and carefully chosen language that will give the missing information. You need to cut through the vagueness by using specifics and by challenging inaccurate statements that lead to confusion.

The best starting point is to train yourself right now to recognize that people take in data in different ways. They think differently and NLP has established its definition of thinking patterns that they call 'Representational Systems'. By recognizing that this exists, you can raise it to conscious awareness and look out for the clues to ways that other people think.

The main systems are:

1. Visual
2. Auditory
3. Kinaesthetic (Feelings)
4. Auditory Digital

1. Visual

Visual people see things. They prefer to see pictures and they prefer to see things as images, pictures, plans or diagrams so they will like colour, flipcharts and photographs.

The phrases in the language pattern of visual people will include:

♦ I see what you mean
♦ Looks good to me
♦ Appears to me
♦ Well defined
♦ Mental picture
♦ Paint a picture
♦ Mind's eye
♦ Gain a perspective
♦ Plainly seen
♦ See to it
♦ Reveal the facts
♦ Show the data
♦ Bring it into focus

- Take a snapshot
- Gain a clear picture

2. Auditory

Auditory people hear things. Sound is their preferred medium to interface with the world so they may hear words rather than see them on the page, they may learn better through music and through talking things through. Silence will be a barren place for them.

Recognize when you are speaking to an auditory person by listening intently for their language patterns that might include some of the following:

- Rings a bell
- Sounds right to me
- I hear what are you saying
- This has a certain resonance for me
- Music to my ears
- Tuning in to you
- Describe in detail
- Idle chat
- Being heard
- Announcing news
- It is unheard of
- Voicing an opinion

3. Kinaesthetic

Kinaesthetics are people who enjoy touch, physical contact and tangible evidence. They like to taste, to smell and to have the evidence of what is there before them. A trainer I know visits Paperchase, the stationery supplier, before her training sessions and buys crazy pens, pencils, erasers and squeezy gadgets to put on the table for her delegates. She watches who uses them and instantly knows her kinaesthetics from her auditories.

Other clues to kinaesthetics will be found in their language patterns too. Look out for:

♦ Grasping the facts
♦ Staying in touch
♦ Getting a feel of the situation
♦ Laying my cards on the table
♦ Working hand in hand
♦ It slipped my mind
♦ Let's touch base
♦ Feeling light headed
♦ Catching on to the facts
♦ Building on firm foundations
♦ Tapping into the network
♦ Rubbing up the wrong way

4. Auditory Digital

Auditory Digital people like to make sense of the world through steps, procedures and sequences. They are likely to have internal debates with themselves and may in fact catch themselves talking to themselves. Internal dialogue is constantly happening. They like things to make sense and will flit across the other representational systems, buying into a bit of everything, so long as it helps create the structure that they need.

Words they may favour will include:

♦ Understand
♦ Distinct
♦ Experience
♦ Clarity
♦ Structure
♦ Think
♦ Learn
♦ Understand

What about you?

Before you start exploring the thinking style of others, first of all know yourself. The best way to improve your dealings with people in your business is to start by working out what your preferred way of thinking is. Here are some statements for you to consider that will pave the way to self-knowledge. Read the statement, ask yourself 'Is this a close fit for me?' and then write yes or no.

	Statement	Yes / No
1.	I make my decisions based on hunches and instincts	
2.	I like to share my feelings with others	
3.	I love to touch things and am sensitive to the textures in my life	

	Statement	Yes / No
4.	I make sure I am in touch with the feelings of others in the team	
5.	I often think about how things look to me	
6.	I communicate strongly by what I wear and how I look	
7.	I can often see someone else's point of view	
8.	I respond strongly to the way my environment looks and the colours used	
9.	I am very in tune with the sounds around me	
10.	In discussions I am influenced by the tone of voice of the other person	
11.	I make decisions by knowing what sounds best	
12.	People can tell what I am thinking by the tone of my voice	
13.	I communicate by careful choice and use of words	
14.	I like making sense of things through facts and data	
15.	I decide by focusing on an analysis of the facts around issues	
16.	I am influenced by the sound logic of another person's debate	

YES: Questions 1–4 – these are all the preferences of kinaesthetic people. If you have endorsed these, then you like to be intuitive and you will listen to a gut instinct. This K preference can leave others around you a little mystified about the reasons for your thoughts and decisions

YES: Questions 5–8 – these are all the preferences of people who are highly visual. If you have endorsed these, then you are likely to see the world in pictures and to get bored by long-winded discussions that are only words. Your PowerPoint will always have pictures, colour, logos and graphics. For you, there is more to life than just words and numbers.

YES: Questions 9–12 – these are the preferences of people who have an auditory preference. You will be someone who can be distracted by noise around you and you like to learn by listening. You will like to chat in person and on the phone and you probably have music around you. You will be attuned to the tone of voice that others use.

YES: Questions 13–16 – these are the preferences of Auditory Digital people, the ones who like an analytical structure around what they do. You will like an objective data-driven basis for your decisions and you are likely to wander across the other representational systems, so you will be using feeling, thinking, hearing and seeing in order to get to the right answer.

Count up your yes responses to the statements and you will then start to formulate a picture of where your preferences lie.

Other people

Now that you have insights into the lens that you use to look at the world, consider other people. Begin right now to look out for clues in their language. When you know how they prefer to interface with the world, make it easier for them by using their language of choice. Be kinaesthetic for people whose thinking patterns are like that. By being aware of how people prefer to think, you will be extending your own flexibility and your influence and this ability to adapt to differing circumstances is what will add to the value of your communication. You will feel more in touch and you will hear what is happening around you, seeing what you need to do next and deciding about it in a structured and objective way. Detecting the thinking style of others is the first step towards walking in someone else's shoes. Integrate this into your rapport building techniques and you will be an assured and accomplished performer in the business. If you still remain unsure, incorporate all of the representational systems into your language pattern, For example, you could say 'I can see what you mean by this and I can detect the difference in tone in the statistics and data you are providing. This all rings bells for me and I can feel that we are heading in the right direction.'

Make the decision now to become observant. If you are already sharp eyed and someone who spots things, decide to fine tune that skill even further. Notice details about people and the environment. For example, think of a meeting you were in recently and remember who was there and what they were wearing. Imagine you have to describe them to a stranger. How much detail can you remember? Now recall one key favourite phrase that they used. Now think of what the room looked like, the pictures on the walls, the colour of the chairs.

Be ready to identify patterns about language so you can be ready to make accurate assumptions about their preferred way of thinking ('modalities' if you want the proper NLP term). Listen hard, look hard and notice things that you normally wouldn't. Reflect on what you hear and what you see. What could it mean and how can you alter your behaviour to accommodate it? For example if you detect that someone has a visual preference, become like that yourself. Use the same language patterns and you are already one step ahead. Working from the premise that the most flexible person controls the system, become the one to work well with the difference of others that you have been smart enough to spot.

One of my clients was Fiona, HR Manager of a UK based engineering business, who was convinced that her boss was making the wrong decision about redundancies. Although she accepted that costs needed to be cut and that jobs had to be sacrificed, she did not agree with the list that the MD had pulled together. She believed that the business would suffer if he made the Sales Director, Tim, redundant and if he relied on the efforts of the sales team alone. Her preferences were kinaesthetic and her opening argument to him was along these lines 'I feel we are making the wrong decision here. I have worked closely with Geoff for some time now and what he is doing is based on solid foundations. I worry that the team will lose a leader and they will feel out of touch and out of alignment. They rely on Tim and his style of management that is in tune with their needs. I feel we need to rethink this and do what would be best to maintain such a harmonious team that is in touch with marketplace.'

Geoff, Auditory Digital, was not impressed by arguments that seemed to him to lack logic and a framework that would help the business achieve its goals. His response was along the lines of 'I have looked at all of the facts and analysed the sales figures of the last 12 months. While Tim is doing a good job in a difficult marketplace, he has failed to secure the sales volumes and the margins we need and is now an expensive overhead we cannot afford.'

These two people were not connecting at any level. For Fiona to get through to him, she needed to present her arguments in Auditory Digital language that Geoff would value. Had she said 'I have analysed the sales data for the last twelve months and it is clear to me that Tim's input is high energy and high impact. I have looked at the sales pipeline and I have identified five major contracts that will be at risk if we let him go. Retaining him in the business will add profit in the short term, new contracts in the long and will bring much needed stability to a young team.' This response is reasoned and logical, relying on facts.

The attributes of the ideal employees will be explored in turn and I will put them under the NLP spotlight. You may choose to work your way quickly and thoroughly through the chapters one by one or you may wish to start with what you do best, to understand why it is that you are good at doing what you do. You may wish to start with the one that you feel least comfortable with and start to understand how you plan to change. It is up to you. There are many routes to success so choose the one that suits you best.

Remember: there is no failure, only feedback. Use this as a step towards greatness and make the change to acceptance of the feedback of others as well as willingness to share your own constructive feedback with them.

Positive Attitude

HOW TO DEVELOP THE MINDSET THAT GIVES YOU THE POSITIVE OUTCOME

"People have all the resources they need to succeed"

This cornerstone of NLP thinking is one of the most empowering. You can do whatever you like if you believe it. If you want it enough, you will find a way. You have got what you need to get the results you need; all you have to do is to know how to use your skills. Businesses succeed because of the innate belief that people can do what they say they are going to do. If your starting point is a lurking fear that you may fail the exam or not win the order, you have given away some of your power. Utter self-belief, even when it would seem to be flying in the face of facts, will always win the day.

> **John Dargan, entrepreneur and global business leader, says:**
>
> 'I look for the right attitude... Specifically I look for people who are prepared to take on responsibility and be accountable for it. I like people who want to be clearly measured and who understand what success is. I look for that optimistic, can do, 'never say die' attitude that convinces me they will do what they commit to ... every time'

Utter self-belief

How would you like to be surrounded by cheerful people who seem to have a solution to everything? Constructive and positive people who can reconstruct any situation so that there is a solution rather than a problem are welcome in any company, so long as it based on realism rather than on senseless optimism. If you want to be valued as a positive and committed team member who matches a positive attitude with a consistent delivery of performance, then take the time to inject new self-belief and certainty into your daily work.

I once interviewed someone for a Sales Director position and I was very dubious about him before I even started. He cancelled two meetings and I questioned whether or not he was really interested. A third interview was arranged and he was not off to the greatest start.

When I met him he instantly took control of the situation. He had prepared an outstanding PowerPoint presentation about himself and the company I was recruiting for. He had used every ounce of his skills to produce a high quality piece of work and this was matched by his complete certainty that he was the right man for the job. This combination gave him a focus that was hard to deflect. He got the job and transferred his positive certainty to business development in his new job.

Using NLP techniques to develop a more positive outlook will mean that you are enabling choice in your life, creating the life that you want rather than coping with the life that you have ended up with.

Pura Vida

Some people seem to be those who generate energy and they impart this physical enabling to others. They are vibrant, enthusiastic and terrific to be around. They raise the game in all the people around them so that their energy by being shared seems to be multiplied. In Costa Rica when people meet each other they say, 'Que tal?', meaning 'How are you?' The standard and automatic response is 'Pura Vida', meaning 'It's a great life'. People who have a natural belief that it is Pura Vida are those who will find what they expect.

However, beware the energy drainers and the energy blockers, the ones who see trouble everywhere and who leave you deflated, depressed and wishing you had never spent any time with them. How do you protect yourself from the negative energy of others?

Gareth James, Director of People Plus, said:

'Always be positive – even when saying negative things!
– it takes 10 'can do's to recover from 1 'can't do' – nega-
tivity drains others of energy and de-motivates them to
work with you.'

Starting off with positive intent

Whenever you embark on anything, start with the expectation
of success. Recognizing that life can be a self-fulfilling prophecy, create your own future by the way that you set off.

Decide what you are going to do in order to give out a more
positive message. Think about what you say when people say
'How are you?' I am prepared to bet that you have some kind
of stock response. Decide here and now that the stock response
has gone forever. Choose how you are going to be perceived
by others and decide that you will always be seen to be positive, upbeat, and enthusiastic. This is not in a brittle, superficial
way but by telling your unconscious mind continuously that
you are feeling brilliant and raring to go, it will become a fact.
It is easy to slip into careless ways with language so remembering that the person with the greatest flexibility is the one who
rules, challenge yourself to be different.

This positive attitude and expectation applies to projects,
plans, trainings and seminars that form part of your work. The
next time you are invited to a conference, a training course a
seminar, make the starting point, 'This will be great and I will

learn something from it.' If you are meeting new colleagues or new customers, before the meeting frame the thought that 'I am sure they will have valuable experience to bring to the business and they will have something good to offer.' When you are sitting an exam, know that you will pass and do well.

After all, if you think that things are going to be a waste of time, you will usually find what you expect. Change the nature of your expectation into something that carries with it hope and a sense of optimism. Model it. Think of someone you know who is cheerful and has the knack of turning everything into an opportunity rather than a path full of pitfalls. Listen for the language that they use and watch what they look like. Then do it too.

Thomas Edison said:

'I have not failed 700 times. I have not failed once. I have succeeded in proving that those 700 ways will not work. When I have eliminated the ways that will not work, I will find the way that does work.'

The magic of positive language

Begin every conversation and every piece of communication with the assumption that you will succeed and that you will get what you are looking for. When you are considering your approach, 'act as if' you will succeed. This means that the language you use needs to be clean and precise, leaving no room for doubt, the enemy of the positive thinker, to creep in.

For example, 'if' is not a helpful word to get you what you want. To say 'if I achieve my sales number' is much less powerful than 'When I achieve my sales number.' 'If you decide to place the business with me' does not work nearly as well as 'When you decide to place the business with me.' This subtlety of language works in two ways. It is convincing your own unconscious mind that it is a reality, and it also slips this certainty into the mind of the person you are talking to. The unconscious mind cannot absorb a negative and is the servant of the conscious mind with the duty of following orders. This means that when you issue the instruction 'When I receive the promotion' and 'when I hit my deadline', this is perceived to be a reality.

When working with colleagues or customers or suppliers, the way to encourage a positive response to your ideas and proposals is to couch them in the kind of language that will mean that you are predisposed to listen and to accept. Construct the kind of phraseology that will help you, for example, try including some of the following:

♦ Knowing it is the right thing
♦ Considering all of its benefits
♦ That you can learn
♦ You probably are aware
♦ I know that you are wondering
♦ Accepting the benefits of
♦ Welcoming new approaches

Using this positive language that assumes acceptance will break down barriers that might stand between you and success. The best people in the organization are winners. They expect to win and they bounce back in the face of setbacks.

Goal setting is something that everyone will be faced with sooner or later. Someone asks you what you are going to achieve and you have to put your name either to a sales number or a date, for example when you are going to have accomplished certain tasks. No one will thank you for being cautious and giving a number or a date that is not in some way a stretch for you. Now is the time to be brave, to be positive and to establish a goal and an expectation that is positive. As a client of mine tells his team, 'Success is not not failing.' Whilst you do not want to stack yourself up for failure and thus to be responsible for the fall out on other areas of the business, you can use this time to set up two expectations. One will be an optimistic number or deadline that will be achieved if every-thing goes well. The other date or number will be still be an aspirational figure but will be one that provides an expectation that circumstances change. The real key to success is for your personal goal to be to set out with the belief and conviction that you can achieve the well nigh impossible. Winners in a business are those with the belief that they will be successful.

A positive reframe

Some people have an extraordinary skill in turning situa-tions round and altering their reactions to something that is potentially damaging into a positive context. By doing this you are changing the framework around the event.

NLP practitioners set great store by the desire to Reframe, an ability to make a shift in the nature of a problem. All meaning is context dependent. It follows, therefore, that if you change the context or the content, then you will change the meaning. Great people in business are able to alter contexts, process or structure so that whatever happens can be moved from a negative to a positive meaning and outcome.

By consistently representing your experiences so that they lead to greater results, you will be empowered to have better results. Surely this is the key to having a positive and more successful career? Wouldn't you just love to have the skill to turn every situation round in order to find a benefit? An example of finding a positive could be when someone resigns from your team. One way to look at it is to realize that it will leave a large hole in the team, meaning that there could be an impact on sales and that the business is likely to take some kind of financial hit. A positive reframing of this situation could be that change is always a good thing and this will allow others in the team to grow their skills and take on more responsibilities. This will mean that they are more motivated, eager to show how much more they can do and perhaps it could be a chance to take someone off the shop floor and train them up.

NLP working for you

I travelled recently in the US with a client and I marvelled at how he managed to improve his travel conditions. He was upgraded on every flight, he was moved from an executive room to a suite in the hotel and he had the world revolving around him. It seemed as though everyone was working to make sure that this pretty tough business trip was one that was going to be more comfortable for him than for anyone else. How did he do it?

His starting point was his clear goal. He was going to travel in the greatest comfort possible and with the highest levels of customer service being used to help him along. He was restricted by his company's tight rules on expenses so he could not use his credit card to buy what he wanted. He had to rely on his attitude and belief that people willingly choose to give more. As a consequence of a smoother and more comfortable travel plan, he was better rested and his performance in front of customers and suppliers had a greater sparkle.

How did he do it and how do you utilize those talents to achieve the same thing?

1. A goal

He had a clearly established goal. He knew exactly what he wanted and he set it with clarity and determination. His experience led him to do this naturally so, recognizing that modelling excellence is at the heart of NLP, how do you achieve the same results? Model his goals, his attitudes and his outcomes to bring other elements of your life under your own control. Here's the strategy for you to model:

♦ State your goal in positive terms. 'I want to travel so I am rested and relaxed and ready to do a great day's work.' It would not work if you said 'The last thing I want to do is to get stuck in economy class and have a terrible journey.' Delete that from your thinking and whatever your goal might be, ensure that it is set in a positive framework.

♦ It must be something that you have decided that you want and not what someone else thinks you need. You will initiate the goal and you will maintain it.

♦ It must have a purpose that is ecological and be a force for good. Winning the lottery won't work and getting away with a bank heist won't either.

♦ Accept that there could be more than one way to get the result you want. If we stick with the travel example, it might be that you have a seat empty next to you in economy so you have more space and you travel better.

♦ Make sure that the first step is clearly specified and achievable

♦ And does it increase choice in your life? The best conditions for achieving the goals in your life mean that it adds value to what you do and gives you different options.

2. Rapport

Our role model traveller was someone who had a natural ability to establish rapport. His approach was flexible and his focus was on matching and mirroring the people he was dealing with. The purpose of his communication was not to check in, it was to establish clear communication on the right wave length with the person at the check in desk.

If you want to be someone with this kind of impact, find a role model and practise your skills in establishing rapport. In summary, as we have covered this in depth elsewhere, get that rapport by:

♦ Matching – doing exactly the same as the person you are talking to. That means you match their right with your right and their left with your left.

♦ Mirroring – acting as though you are looking at a mirror image so their left will be your right and their right will be your left.

♦ Posture – stand in the same way and hold your head in the same way.

♦ Hand movements – watch how they move their hands when they talk and do the same, initially smaller versions of what they do and gradually increasing to the same level of expansiveness.

♦ Facial expressions – watch for how much they want to maintain eye contact and make sure you stay in the same levels. Notice how often they blink and do the same.

♦ Breathing – notice the kind of breathing they do, whether it is light, shallow, deep, fast, and slow and breathe in the same way.

♦ Speech – match the speech so that your voice shares the same tone, speed, timbre and volume. Look out for how people end their sentences and finish off in the same way that they do.

♦ Words – look for whether they are using auditory vocabulary, kinaesthetic, or

♦ Key words – if they favour a certain word pattern or exclamation, introduce them all into your language too.

These techniques will mean that you are positive about what you are going to do and how you are going to do it. It is another way of ensuring that you are in control of your world and able to harness skills you didn't know you had in order to improve your environment for an excellent performance.

Motivation

You can have all of the techniques and toolkits in the world to help you at work and at home. People can be eager to help and ready to give you the skill and the knowledge to get the promotion or the success you are seeking. However, motivation is a door locked from the inside. No one can want you to do something. If it is going to be done, then it will be done because you want it. You also cannot want something for someone else. Some people are happy with the job they have and they are living life as they want to live it. They don't want change and they don't seek difference. Their motivation is to stay with what they have. Others are ambitious for the next move, more responsibilities, greater power, better working conditions, more money. Wherever you sit on the spectrum of motivation, check also where you sit on the scale of complacency. The job for life, if it ever existed, has gone. The constant pressure of reducing costs and increasing profits means that business overheads are kept under constant review. Continuously improving your performance at work will mean that you are a vital part of the business.

Motivated people generally have a positive outlook. Motivation means working towards achieving something. A different kind of motivation is the one where the impetus is to get away from something so they are trying to get away from something that they wish to avoid.

Positive people are likely to have a 'towards' attitude, one that is driving you towards something that is life enhancing. You could be working in this job because you want to be the next Chief Executive, or because you want to make huge bonuses. You might be doing it because it gives you a great life balance and it helps you be happier and healthier. These potentially exciting benefits are the positive drivers for people.

On the other hand, 'away from' people are motivated by a desire to avoid something. This could be that they are working to avoid the alternative, which is being jobless and poor or it could be that they are avoiding the risk of doing something that you would prefer to do as they do not want to fail. Many people stick in the job they are doing as they do not want to risk rejection by failing at the selection interview or they may fear failure in a new role. 'Away from' people can be perceived to be negative by their buoyant and positive colleagues and yet their warning voice and their caution can sound the alert about possible traps ahead. The whole insurance market could be considered one of avoidance and 'away from' but without insurance we would all at some point have come unstuck.

Think about your motivation to identify the source of your motivation. Ask yourself 'Why did you choose that role?', 'Why did you choose to move to that company?', 'Why did you choose to follow that course of study?' Examine key areas of your life and decide your areas of 'towards' and those that are 'away from'.

How to be a high performer

High performers in organizations are aware of their need to manage their image. It is important to keep recalling, 'How do I impress?' and be sure to demonstrate the right kind of aptitude, attitude and motivation. This will depend on your job context and is bound to include an ability to deliver high quality work to the right deadline, be an excellent team worker and be someone who has positive expectations of others. These may be tempered with a realism that extra resources may be required to get the desired result. Your own performance lies in your own control. However, the results that you deliver will be enhanced or diminished by those around you so what can you do to make sure that you are getting the best out of everyone around you?

Other people's positive performance

Whilst you may feel you have your own goals and expectations under control, it might not be so easy to feel so positive about team members. Here is a strategy to follow to manage your team and the individuals in it:

First step – send the message!

The first key step to gaining an achievable outcome from your colleague is to know what you want specifically to achieve and then to ensure that this message has been effectively and clearly communicated. Be clear about what you want. This is the time to use the precise language of the tiny chunks that make up the whole. There is no room for vague language. Words such as precise, exact, meticulous, date, time, specific, detail are needed. If you are looking for someone to produce a report, make sure you set out the content, the deadline and the key outcomes. Having communicated this, you then will ask 'What specifically do you need to do to deliver the work to me in the form and the timescale I am looking for?' The answer will mean that you are sure that you will get what you need.

Second step – get it done!

The second step is to ask 'Where are you now?', requiring information about what stage the person is at in the process. Another question could be 'Let us imagine that you have done this task and safely delivered it on time and to the right quality, a job well done. Standing in that position, look back and define the hurdles you had to overcome in order to achieve it. Now describe them in chronological order.'

Third step – no mistakes!

The third step is then to be sure that your colleague has all of the resources they need to get there. The question to ask is 'What do you have now and what do you need in order to deliver this piece of work?' This is now the time to ask if they have ever done this kind of thing before or if they know anyone who has and who could assist them.

This carefully laid out process will mean that your positive expectations will be backed up by clarity of purpose – no room for error.

Using Anchors to create a positive state

Even the most positive person has a down moment, a second when they allow negative thoughts to creep in. Research into the attitudes of CEOs showed that many of them had an unreasonable and irrational fear that one day someone would tap them on the shoulder and tell them that it had all been a big mistake and that the job was not meant for them. This is a way of dressing up the insecurity in all of us that just as someone can hire you, they can also fire you.

How do you keep those thoughts at bay and how do you get rid of them if they arrive unbidden and unwanted?

A positive anchor

An anchor is a stimulus that triggers a response in you or others and it can come from any one of the five senses – sight, sound, touch, smell and taste. I will be revisiting the form and the use throughout the book because anchors, used carefully and constructively across a broad range of situations, will give you the power to control your life. When you know something works and instantly puts you in a great mood, what could happen if you used whatever it is in a deliberate way whenever you wanted them to induce those exhilarating moods of confidence and delight? These anchors are physical, auditory and sensory and are individual to you and your life. The sound of the sea crashing on the shore might be inspiring and happy for one person and it could be source of dread for another. Many people have a photo of their nearest and dearest on their desk or bookcase in the office as happy reminders of why they are there and what they are working for. Here are a few suggestions about how you can introduce what is already in your life into your working pattern so that it will keep you focused, keep you positive and allow you to achieve your goals. Great people in a business are consistent in their performance.

1. Music

Make up a CD or a play list of inspiring music. Think of music that brings back happy memories, music that was played at a party or a tune that was on the radio during a particularly happy period of your life. Choose the music that was at your wedding or a concert when you were with friends and the overall memory is of laughter and happiness. Whatever that music is, play it in the car, on your iPod, in the office or on Spotify and invoke the mood. Play it on your way to important meetings, sales pitches or interviews. Play it at times when you feel yourself slipping and your mood darkening. Play it as you sit at your desk in your home office. Whatever feeling that music invoked, be there now.

If you want to create an anchor for others, you could use music as a way of reminding them of you, the team, and the decisions. Lighten the day in the office by starting the meeting with one tune, whatever that is. Play it to signify the start of the Monday sales meeting and whenever your team hears that beat, they will think of sales. Make sure you get the timing right. Use this musical anchor to bring an instant focus to your team. You are creating an unconscious link between the stimulus, that is to say the music, and the event.

2. Tastes and Smells

Certain tastes and certain smells invoke different recollections, both good and bad. I think I only need mention school dinners for the smell of tinned tomatoes and cabbage to be instantly present. Supermarkets are clever at baking fresh bread in their stores as this wonderful smell is inviting and delicious, causing customers to spend more money. Here the link between the stimulus and the product is cash generation. Estate agents advise house sellers to put on a fresh pot of coffee when they are showing people around as it creates a positive state that will encourage the potential purchasers to be more disposed to that house than another.

Use these in the workplace and you will be adding positive elements to the working environment that will work well for you. You could do this by bringing cakes or sweet smelling fruit to meetings so that the alluring smell will be linked positively in your colleagues' minds with your agenda. Put flowers in reception or your office and use everything you have to encourage the positive mindset that will get extra results from your team.

Equally, if you have got your squash gear lying in the corner of the office, or a few mouldy oranges in a bowl, remove them right now. Make your environment an inviting one that conjures up warm images and positive associations.

Convince yourself and convince others

Positive thinking on a flimsy base is no good to anyone as it won't be sustained. In order for it to be more than empty words or an attitude, you need to be convinced that it is right. Other people may tell you that you can do something and you may choose to believe them. Some people need more convincing than this and this may include you. How do you convince others and convince yourself and therefore change to a positive attitude?

The first step is to ask yourself, how do you know when someone else is good at their job?

Do you have to:

1. See it
2. Hear it
3. Read it
4. Do it

Once you know how it is that you decide, you will then be able to use the same question to work out how that other person measures competence at work. Do they use the same thinking process as you or is it different? If it is different then you need to change your approach to convince. You can set the right context for getting into rapport with them by using the right language that they will listen to, read, see or do. You are using their way of thinking and therefore you are more likely to be believed.

Now that you have worked this out, how many times does someone have to demonstrate competence to you in order for you to be convinced? Are you automatically convinced? Do you need to see it a number of times? Does it have to happen over a period of time or perhaps what you are looking for is consistency? Once the right context has been established, you know what needs to happen for you to be truly convinced and for you to have the belief in a positive outcome. Now you need to be aware of the people around you. How are they convinced and how often do they have to demonstrate competence before they are convinced?

To check that you have achieved the right outcome you can ask:

'Can you do it now?'
'How do you do it?'
'How do you know that the problem has disappeared?'

I knew a Chief Executive of a start-up business who was considering making further investment in new capital equipment that was capable of increasing the turnover of the business with significantly added margin. He asked his Finance Director who gave him all the data that he needed to be sure it was the right thing to do. He did not make the decision. He then met a friend at the golf club and they chatted about it as they played a game, talking about it in all its perspectives as they went across the golf links. He still did not make the decision. He then went to the factory floor and as he walked round, watching the processes take place, he took the time to sit down and discuss the investment with his Production Manager. He then decided to invest and was positive that it would be successful and that he had made the right decision. This man needed to be convinced in three different ways to reach a positive outcome.

Remember: you have all the resources you need to succeed. All you need to do is to recognize them, grow them and use them.

Confidence

HOW TO GROW THE CONFIDENCE TO ACHIEVE YOUR GOALS

"If what you are doing is not working, try something different"

A prime quality of a high achiever is that of confidence. People who are confident tend to achieve more than those who are not. If you want to be the person at work who is looked to as a leader, then you need to have self-belief and you need to be seen to be confident by others. If you are not naturally confident, then build your confidence through a number of ways. Confidence comes from within and is a state of mind. No one can give it to you but other people can erode it. Your kind of confidence will be worked at initially, developed and grown through consistent effort and then will become a habit. Growing the habit of self-confidence will allow you to surround yourself with people who listen to you and who respect your view point. Influence and authority are natural outcomes of a confident demeanor.

You will find that persuading others will be easier when you are seen to be confident. This quality will spill over into every area, making it easier to make decisions, easier to take people with you and will enhance your reputation.

If you are looking for promotion and greater responsibilities, you need to believe in it yourself. It is just as important to encourage confidence in those around you. Confident business leaders surround themselves with people who have great self-belief and who know they can deliver results.

Better than a bookmark - something to help through the book

A Windscreen wiper

Before we begin, please provide yourself with a large windscreen wiper, the kind that you see on state of the art articulated lorries. The way to clear irritating images and thoughts and noises that keep repeating themselves in your mind is to use that windscreen wiper and get rid of everything in sight. When unwelcome sounds, words and images pop up, close your eyes and imagine a large windscreen wiper clearing the screen, removing everything that is hampering you from seeing clearly. Do it now. Better? Be ready to use that windscreen wiper when you need to so that you can stay in control of what you are thinking, feeling, hearing and seeing.

Seeing your success

Most people are seeking confidence in speaking to groups, making decisions, making uncomfortable calls, challenging others, selling, being interviewed or negotiating. Sit in a quiet place and imagine yourself in the first context that you identified as one where you need more confidence. Run a scene in your mind that takes you through the situation in a positive way where you are successful. Now do it again. This time make it bigger, add in colour, hear what is being said around you and play it through to the same successful outcome. Do it again until it runs seamlessly from beginning to end. This visualization of success will lull the unconscious mind into a position of confidence, believing that it has already been achieved.

The Posture of Confidence

You can't be confident if your posture is wrong. Your body reflects what you are thinking so consider this. Stand in a droopy way, head down as if you are ready to give in. Keeping your head down and without smiling say in a dull monotone! 'I am feeling glad to be alive.' Now, give yourself a shake, apply the windscreen wiper, and put your shoulders back. Straighten up and hold your head high. Put a smile on your face and say in a bright cheerful tone 'I am feeling absolutely miserable today.' Neither of these scenarios worked did they? The link between your physical demeanour and your expression of your feelings is a strong one and can have an impact on each other. In order to gain greater control over your state of mind, be aware of what you look like to others.

If you are preparing to go into a meeting with people you don't know, don't like or distrust, or if you are preparing for an appraisal with your boss and dreading the discussions, make your starting point a physical statement about your mindset. You will be upright, head up and purposeful. Your outward expression will be that of someone who is confident, upbeat, positive and with energy. It is important to maintain this during the meeting so be aware that you need to keep asking yourself 'How do I appear to the people in this room?' Imagine you are a spectator. Come outside yourself and be what people would love to be, a fly on the wall. Settle somewhere near the ceiling and look down on the room. What do you see? Look closely at the people and decide if they are reflecting what they should. Would you change anything? If you would, what would it be? Look closely at yourself and decide what you can do to give the confident air that you need.

When you are attending a meeting with your team, ensure that you all are matching and mirroring each other's posture. Orders have been lost and deals have disappeared because of the wrong message being sent in a room.

I was working with a high performing, highly profitable business that was up for sale and the board of directors was interviewing potential purchasers. One team arrived, the preferred choice of the board based on telephone calls and e mails. The potential investors then spent the meeting checking their Blackberrys and losing focus in the meeting. They failed to give the board of directors the confidence in them that they were looking for and were excluded from the bid process.

And the good thing about that ... Reframing

As we saw in the previous chapter, some people just seem to have the skill to see situations in a different and a more positive light. For them it comes naturally but others have to work at it. The skill of truly confident people is their ability to readjust how they think about what has happened to them. How do you react if your boss tells you the planned training has been cancelled? What if a project you have dedicated hours to and is almost completed is now declared to be cancelled and surplus to requirements? You have a few options here. You can complain, feel hard done by, be disappointed, blame others, decide it is all a waste of time and feel diminished and less confident about yourself and your ability. This is potentially turning what is a set back into a disaster. Alternatively, you can decide to change your mindset to one that seeks out possible benefits and positives, using it to increase your confidence and not diminish it.

Reframing is a technique to look at situations in a different way. It starts with the question 'How else can I consider this or how else can I do this? What is it that you have not noticed about this situation that will bring about a different meaning and change your response?' NLP is about choice, about how you choose to see situations and then how you react to them. You can't change what happens to you but you can change how you react.

The biggest pressure in recent years has been dealing with cuts in staff in businesses. It is tough for people who leave the business and have to find a new path in life. It is equally tough for those who remain with the business, facing the same volumes of work but with reduced resources. Expectations will be greater and the pressures will be increasing. A natural reaction could be: 'Life is going to be impossible without the right people and this round of redundancies is going to mean we will never get through the work.' This expectation is setting you up for failure whereas a different framework could be: 'This is an opportunity for me to show how good I am. I will be able to persuade others to move to slicker ways by using more technology and successes in a difficult market will be valued more than they would have been when things were buoyant.'

The facts remain the same but the framework around the events has changed.

Limiting beliefs

The biggest block to your progress is not other people and it is not the environment in which you are working. The biggest single limiting factor in your development is what you believe about yourself. Whatever you believe, it is true for you. How many times have you caught yourself saying 'I am hopeless at' … whatever it might be. Beliefs turn into reality so the route from good to great is to ensure that you are empowered by a positive building belief rather than a limiting one.

Sometimes our upbringing, our family and our friends can have a positive impact on what we believe about ourselves and our capabilities. Other people's humour can be damaging, reminding you of occasions when you were not at your best, made a mistake, spilt coffee in a meeting or called someone by the wrong name. It can also be damaging when people remember you from a different time in your life before you gained the skills you have today. It is easy to develop limiting beliefs about yourself and your capabilities. It is equally easy to challenge them and to break through the self imposed boundaries. Just because you were hopeless at maths when you were 15 does not mean you are not capable of being highly numerate now. You might not have been creative when you were five but you may have developed a more artistic outlook and capability now. Different place, different person, different motivation. This applies equally to the people who work with and for you. What are you going to do to challenge their limiting beliefs?

Remember that these beliefs are often based on emotion rather than facts so this could present a bit of a conflict when decisions are made in the workplace based on objective evidence of what you do and what you contribute. You might find this to be at odds with what you believe about yourself. The trouble is, you might be projecting your limiting belief about what you are capable of into the workplace and this might have an unnecessary adverse impact. For example, if you believe that you are hopeless at organizing things, then people will believe this about you and not ask you to get involved. Likewise, if you believe that most people are easy to get on with and want to do a good job, you will probably find what you expect. If you believe that most people are out to get you, then life will become a self-fulfilling prophecy.

Think of five core beliefs that you have about yourself, about others and about how you view the world.

1.

2.

3.

4.

5.

Now review them. If they are supportive and empowering, giving you the fuel to do well, keep them. If they are restrictive then decide now that you will discard them. Perhaps the best role model is an entrepreneur I know who said when asked what beliefs he might have held that could have restricted his personal growth, replied 'I have always struggled because I have never had a single limiting belief in my life. I think I can do anything.'

When you look at your colleagues, reflect on what you might have thought about them, that they are not good at negotiating, that they have hit the limit of their capabilities or are not able to take the next step. Often people leave organizations as they have hit some form of barrier, often because companies cannot see them in a broader role. When they transplant into a new environment where people have not preconceived notions about what they are able to do, they often shine. Apprentices used to find that they had to move from their company two or three years after qualifying as they were always seen as the apprentice who made the tea. Make sure you are not losing the talent in your organization because you are failing to recognize it and value it.

Developing others

Take the responsibility yourself to help others improve their performance. Use carefully formulated questions to find out what is holding someone back. If, for example, you found that someone was reluctant to take a customer facing role, ask them 'What is holding you back from making this move to a customer facing role? What do you believe about yourself that is stopping you and limiting you?'

They may be thinking 'I am not good enough' or 'I don't know enough about the company's products' or 'I am hopeless in front of people I don't know'. This will then give you the opportunity to get them to move from this negative position to a more positive one by asking 'What would be a more empowering belief about your capabilities in front of customers that would be the positive opposite of what you currently believe about yourself?' At this point you stick with this line of questioning until you get answers that have a positive framework such as 'I could do this when I have learnt more about products' or 'I do know how to talk to people' 'Once I have established a bit of rapport, I tend to get on well with people.'

You will now have moved your colleagues to a more empowering belief about themselves and they will be able create ideas about themselves that will allow them to move forward. For example, you could ask 'So knowing that you do know how to talk to people and that you can find out enough about the products, what ideas do you now have that will help you to move into this customer facing role?

Use this structure as a template to refresh your views and opinions about others around you, asking them what more they can do.

Building a confident team

A confident team will create better results than a team that is full of self-doubt and nervousness. It is possible to create an atmosphere that is conducive to failure or limited success by what you and your team believe about yourselves and your capabilities. It is equally possible to create the success you aspire to as individuals and as a team.

Winning teams believe they are winners. They are not people who are saying one thing but are secretly expecting the worst. When they set ambitious goals and targets, they are not simultaneously applying any restrictions by saying or thinking that they might not get there. Winning teams do not say:

Let's try – they either do it or they don't do it. They don't try.

Don't worry – As the unconscious mind cannot take in a negative, there is a message being blasted out that is saying; WORRY! Winning teams do not invite in the option of worrying.

We might not hit the target: Whatever is going on around them, they all act as if they will get where they need to be.

July and December are always bad months in our business: They dismiss statements that mean the starting point is failure.

It is impossible to ….: Winning teams think they can do anything.

You can never ….: These statements of the absolute are unknown to teams who get things done.

You can't beat the market: Winners create their own reality and are unconcerned about the potential impact of others on their own success.

A highly successful entrepreneurial client of mine believes that the best people are those who are first and foremost goal orientated. This is what he looks for in everyone he employs, right across the organization. As a result his team is single-minded, focused and determined both personally and corporately, to deliver what they have promised.

Playing it in your mind

Remembering that the mind and body are connected with delightfully blurred edges, it is time for you to create strong beliefs in yourself. Think of three contexts in which you would like to be more confident and write them down below:

1.
2.
3.

Swish Patterns: Another compelling way to create a confident self

Step One

Think of a time when you were in a situation when you were nervous. It might have been when you had to meet someone and you were unsure of yourself. It could be meeting your new boss, it might be pitching to a potential new customer. It could be standing on an exhibition stand, talking constantly to new people. It could be a business breakfast meeting where you look around the room and you realize that you know no one. It might be the weekly management meeting where you have to speak in front of colleagues. Whatever the situation is, think of where you were, what you wore, what you said and what the voice in your head was saying and how it was sounding.

Step Two

Now think of a time when you were completely confident. It might have been in those magical moments when you learnt to swim, it could be when you passed your driving test, when you took control of a difficult situation. It could be that moment when you knew you had the answer and no one else did, it could be when you won a piece of business. It could be the moment when you found out you had been offered the job that you have now. Take time now to think back to that time. Where were you located? What were you wearing? Who was in the room with you? Who was speaking? Remember that occasion with total clarity. If your picture of it is hazy, bring it into sharper focus. Make it full of colour and hear the sounds of conversation around you. Did your inner voice, that little voice that goes in your head , have anything to say? What was it saying? How was it sounding? Strong? Positive and encouraging? Move on now to remember those feelings that accompanied your success. How did you feel? Happy? Elated? Skilful? Knowledgeable? In control? Whatever those feeling were, remember them now and be there now in that fulfilling moment of your life when you were confident. Hold onto those moments of confidence and remember what they feel like. Make the situation where you were confident bright, intense and compelling. How big is it? Make it bigger, brighter and more colourful with the happy sounds of that confident situation.

Step Three

Bring back the picture of the situation where you were lacking confidence. Now step into it and see it all through your own eyes, meaning you are fully associated with it.

Step Four

Now insert into the lower left hand corner a small, dark picture of the confident situation.

Step Five

Simultaneously shrink that picture of the lacking confidence situation and make it recede to a distant point while simultaneously the small dark picture of the confident state explodes into full colourful view. For even more effect, try doing it with a SWISH sound. Don't be inside that final picture but be dissociated from it.

Read it carefully, have a mental practice run and then do it for real. Make sure you clear the screen of your mind in between SWISH explosions by applying your mental windscreen wiper.

Repeat this action at least three times or more if you need to and discover that you now know how to become confident at those crucial moments when you need all of the resources you can muster.

Confidence and selling

Confident people know how to sell and it is inevitable that at some point you will need to sell something. Some interviewers still use that horrible old ploy in an interview of saying 'Sell me this pen' (or phone or whatever comes to hand), leaving you with a desperate need for a sales strategy. You may need to convince someone to follow your plan, make some investment or even just allow you a long weekend off work. We all sell directly or indirectly so let's make sure we have a strategy that will work. Everything works better with a plan.

Let's imagine you are in a situation with a potential customer. Here are the five simple stages you need to go through in order to get agreement.

1. Establish rapport. Without this, you will get nowhere so focus on all of the matching, mirroring, physiology, voice tones, breathing and language patterns and vocabulary that you need to. Make it a deep rapport so there is a true connection.
2. Ask questions about why someone would want this: 'For what purpose would you want this pen, this car, this service contract?' 'How specifically would you use it?' This is your opportunity to listen intently.

3. This will mean that you will find why they would want it and you have now established a need. You now need to ensure that the customer sees or hears or feels the need to have this item. This is your chance to talk, retaining the rapport and taking them with you. You can play back to them what they have stated as being the purpose of this and incorporating it into your own product and service. For example, 'Hearing that reliability is essential for you and a fundamental part of your contractual requirements, I know you will want to find out about the awards we have won nationally for exactly what is important to you.' This way, you move away from the scripts that have been rehearsed and prepared and instead you are creating a custom built sales pitch.

4. Now link their established need to the product or service you are selling. This is now the time to be making a conditional close that could be phrased 'Is it fair to say that ...' 'What would happen if. ...' 'Because you, ...', thus creating a framework of an agreement.

5. You are there and remember to do what so many people forget – ask for the order!

> Remember: there is no such thing as failure. The path to success, driven by a confident self, is full of lessons that help you to get where you need to be.

6

Energy

HOW TO RISE TO ANY CHALLENGE AND CREATE NEW RESOURCES TO GET THERE

"The mind and body form a linked system"

High calibre people are high energy people. They can race through hectic schedules, power through their e-mails and their 'to do lists.' They always seem to be on the go. They cope with whatever life throws at them and they never seem to be tired. They get involved, they volunteer and they squeeze things in. There is a saying that 'If you want something done, ask a busy person.' It is as if these people have endless founts of energy, a constant supply of battery power than allows them to do more than most people and they seem to be enjoying themselves while they do it. Their energy is almost tangible.

Being around them seems to revive others and put a kick into the whole team.

Rising to the challenge

Businesses want people who can rise to challenges, multi task, run a number of projects, find ways through difficulties and bring back results. High energy people step up to challenges and are the first to see what can be done and they are the ones who want to do it. The most demotivating person in the team is the one who sighs, slumps in their chair, yawns and who is the last person to volunteer. This person drains the energy out of the room, not just by how they look but also by what they say and how they say it. Their starting point in everything seems to be that it will be a trouble, it will be difficult and it will be exhausting. Energy and enthusiasm are closely linked and they become the life-blood of the business.

John Dargan, Entrepreneur and global business leader, is very clear on what is the most important thing to him in his team:

'A passion for success drives the business, it manifests itself in every individual's enthusiastic attitude and approach to everything they do. I look for enthusiasm and passion. I only ever want the A team, I won't compromise on that and to get into the A team you need to demonstrate these types of attributes. I can train the skills to do the job but I can't give you the attitude that motivates you to get out of bed early, to utilize every second of every day to achieve your goals. How do you identify it? Ask them what they did yesterday. Enthusiastic, passionate people have lots going on and they light up when given the chance to talk about what they're doing and why. The secret of success in everything is enthusiasm. Tackle everything you do with enthusiasm and you will succeed. An enthusiastic person rises to the challenge every time.'

Successful people know that in order to achieve their goals, they need to take action. This requires energy so moving from good to great needs a force and a momentum. These are fuelled by resources and some of these will need to be developed and grown.

Resources

When you are thinking of what you need to achieve, ask yourself what you have now and what else you need in order to get your outcome.

Then ask yourself:

♦ Have you ever had or done this before?
♦ Do you know anyone who has?
♦ Can you act as if you have it?

Think of an occasion when you were doing something that you loved and you really enjoyed. It might have been at work and it might be at home. Maybe it was playing football, cooking a meal, riding a bike, mastering a language or chatting on Facebook. Whatever it was, think now of that situation. Recall where you were, what you heard and what you saw. See the picture now and feel the emotions you experienced at the time. Pretend you have it on film and move closer in and see it in brighter colour and sharper detail. Hear the sounds of enjoyment around you. Feel the enthusiasm that you had and that of those around you. Take a snapshot and a sound recording and store them somewhere safe.

Now think of when you wake up in the morning and recall what it feels like. Switch that feeling for the snapshot and the sound recording of the memory before. How much better would it be to feel like that every day and bring that energy to work? Decide right now that every day will bring with it renewed energy and enthusiasm for what you do at work. You are in control of your mind and your actions. No one else is. You can choose to decide that the job you are doing is one that deserves your heightened energetic input. You may decide that it is a means to a different end and that success in this role will give you access to something else that you will value more.

Sarah was a teacher and had been in the profession since she graduated with a brief spell out when she had children. At the age of 46 she decided to resign as she was disillusioned with her job and the way that it had changed over the years. She spent four years at home, not actively job seeking and then realized she needed to get back into full time work because she needed the money. She looked at a few options but decided they were not paying enough money. She didn't want to go back into teaching as she didn't like it. She didn't think she had time to retrain and started to look at administration roles that were way below her level of capability but was rejected. She began to feel that she was out of date and desperately applied for anything but still no luck. She still hasn't got a job.

Why was this? Sarah was overwhelmed by a sense of pessimism and hopelessness. She was disillusioned, disenchanted and resigned to being left behind by life and this was how she was appearing to potential employers. However good her skills and experience were, they were far outweighed by her lack of energy and her pervasive 'flatness'. All people saw was her sense of hopelessness and they simply wanted nothing to do with it.

A source of energy – a Meta Programme

If this high level of energy does not seem to come naturally to you, practicing certain thinking styles will create it for you. One of the key meta programmes that controls behaviour is the source of energy that drives and influences how you behave. A positive force of energy is one where you are doing something because you want to do it and you are moving towards it. This desire to move towards what you want unleashes energy and motivation. You can see what you want and you desire it sufficiently to put every effort into getting there. Eagerness and enthusiasm for what you are doing lends a dynamic force to the activity itself. You will decide that 'A three month secondment to the Birmingham plant will help me grow my network and give me more experience.' The alternative, faced with the inevitable outcome that you have to go anyway, would be to say 'I don't know anyone there and it is going to be lonely and miserable' or 'It is better than being made redundant.' Great people are those who positively choose what they want to do and they choose to find the best in things when faced with the inevitable.

The other kind of behaviour is when you are doing something because you are avoiding something else. Doing something because you want to get away from something is an action that drains energy from the activity. For example, if you agree to go on a Time Management Programme for two days because it is better than being stuck in the office, it will not lead to the same level of success if you had decided that you wanted to do the course, choosing to decide that it would help you be better organized and more efficient.

To replenish stores of energy, decide that the next time you make a decision to do something, it will be positively framed and will be following the path of energy and enthusiasm.

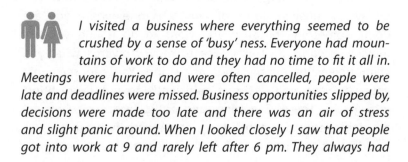

I visited a business where everything seemed to be crushed by a sense of 'busy' ness. Everyone had mountains of work to do and they had no time to fit it all in. Meetings were hurried and were often cancelled, people were late and deadlines were missed. Business opportunities slipped by, decisions were made too late and there was an air of stress and slight panic around. When I looked closely I saw that people got into work at 9 and rarely left after 6 pm. They always had

time for lunch and for coffees. Chatting and moaning about how busy they all were was the constant buzz in the air. Rather than getting on with the job in hand, they seemed to prefer to talk about it. They were not working effectively and they were not prioritizing. If they had got on with the 20% of work effort that would probably make 80% of the difference, they would have achieved something. Being busy is not the same as being energetic.

We often read about people who have survived in apparently impossible circumstances. They have battled through blizzards, survived ship wrecks, shark attacks, deprivation, starvation and circumstances that seem to be insurmountable. The secret of that success is that the power of the mind is stronger than that of the body. By harnessing this energy of the mind, physical weaknesses can be overcome.

The energy of the Universe

How many times have you found yourself in the situation where you have decide to call someone or e-mail and within a very short timescale, that person calls you? Some people put this down to coincidence but in fact it is something more powerful than that. You can, therefore, either decide to stand by and admire it when a coincidence like this occurs or you can choose to create even more of it. This is a good way of getting in touch with people who are perhaps harder to track down than others. For example, if you have been trying to get a customer to call you back with no success, use this method to accelerate contact.

Visualization

Think of the person you want to talk to or e-mail. Bring a picture of their face to mind and make it clear and in full colour. When you have done this, then move your mind's camera lens back so you see them in their environmental context. They might be driving their car, sitting at their desk or sitting in a meeting room. Now hear the sounds of the conversation around them.

If you want to talk to them, picture them picking up the telephone and dialing your number. Stay very focused on their image. If you want them to e mail, picture them sitting at their computer and writing an e mail to you. The stronger your visualization and your belief, the better the message because when you focus on the person, then the communication follows.

Using other people's energy

Energy is not all about racing around. Sometimes the best form of action is inaction. Graham tells the story of how he wanted to find a part-time assistant. He was looking for someone with energy, get up and go who would use their initiative and make things happen. He advertised the role online and he received about 70 responses. He sent an acknowledgement to each one and then he waited. Most people waited too. One person didn't. She e-mailed him, she 'phoned him and she let him know just how keen she was for the job. He met her and employed her and she is a huge success. He believes that she self selected because of the force of her energy.

Using your own energy to stand out

It is not enough to be successful and to do a good job. It is important to be seen to be successful and seen to be doing a good job. This does not mean bringing an apple for teacher or becoming the company creep. This is about the subtle things you need to do to raise your profile. In order for change to happen, change how you project yourself.

If you want to be seen differently then you have to change how you are seen. This is not just suddenly demonstrating a different and dynamic work ethic. It is also looking different, sounding different and behaving differently. How do you achieve this in a subtle and effective way?

♦ **Appearance.** Think about changing your look in small ways so you stop being predictable. If you always wear black, wear red. If you always wear a tie, take it off. Whatever you don't, do and whatever you do, don't.

♦ **Approach.** If you are known for tackling problems through systematic, logical analysis, make sure you add into this an intuitive or creative process. Make the way that you go about your work significantly different and see who notices and how they react.

♦ **Behaviour.** You know how you are seen by others. If you are naturally talkative or quiet, fast paced or methodical, quick to get to the point or always exploring options, whatever it is that you usually are, change it now and then. Use the power of behaving very differently to stop people in their tracks and pay attention. Only use it deliberately and carefully to help you make important points.

◆ **Team.** Look at the team that you manage and decide to bring about innovations in how you manage them. If you usually have meetings on a Monday morning, change the time, change the format and change the venue. Look at everything that you do with your team and inject new energies into it.

◆ **Colleagues.** Look at your relationships inside the organization and take responsibility for increasing their effectiveness. You can do this by changing how you communicate individually and as a group and you can alter the dynamics. If you change in an energetic and positive way, there will be a shift all around.

◆ **Time keeping and input.** Go the extra mile. You can do this in many ways. You can start by making sure that you arrive 5 minutes before and leave 5 minutes after your boss. By being seemingly ever present in the work environment, you are increasing the pace for everyone else around you. Suddenly you are the energetic force in the business.

Internal energy

High energy people are not just the ones racing up and down the motorway, showing that they have stamina and staying power. One of the most powerful forms of energy is an internal one. By focusing on internal energy you will be driving your thought processes and thinking patterns, broadening your ideas and fleshing them out. Barriers to this will be task lists, busy schedules and a frantic pace that excludes quiet time.

Inaction needs to be actively sought out. Opportunities for thinking time could be when you are out running, walking the dog, listening to music or staring out the train window on a long journey. Accept that you are in charge of your life and create the space you need to think.

Decide that you are going to take initially half an hour to stop what you are doing in order to reflect. You don't need an agenda or a list for this. Find a quiet place where you can close the door, turn off the computer, turn off the mobile phone and be on your own. If you have an auditory preference, you can decide to play some music if you like. If you are kinaesthetic, make sure your environment is comfortable and conducive to a pleasant half hour.

Now close your eyes and switch off.

Picture yourself in a pleasant landscape where you feel happy and relaxed. It could be a beach, a country scene or your back garden or anything that gives you a feeling of being relaxed

Use the silence that is around you to empty your mind of busy thoughts. Allow the thoughts to disappear and now you know that you are learning many things. The space will provide you with new insights and new understandings and you will find all the things that you need to know.

Reflection is the secret tool of successful people. Peace, quiet and stillness provide the chance for thoughts to filter through from your unconscious mind, giving you the answers that you knew already but were not aware of.

Make sure that you have scheduled or unscheduled space not to think and you will be adding the resources of untapped internal energies to your role.

External energy

Sometimes it is easier just to churn through work, eradicating mountains of paperwork, clearing inboxes and getting things done. Sometimes the efforts can be patchy meaning that there are inconsistencies in your output and effort. Inevitably it is the inconsistencies that people notice, not the things that have gone well. Turn your energy onto the tasks that get ignored on your list and you will find yourself happier about your work, less likely to worry and you will be better regarded by your boss and your peers.

In my work as a headhunter I met Robert who was the best Sales Director my client had ever had. He built up a good team and he was very externally focused. He was always busy, getting things done and making things happen. One element of his job that he hated was board reports, forecasts and budgets. He wasn't good at PowerPoint and secretly he did not think that monthly detailed reporting mattered. His reasoning was that he was doing what he was paid to do which is managing the sales of the business.

He was told a number of times that his hastily put together presentations that always arrived too late for inclusion in the board pack were having a negative impact on the board. He dismissed these critiques as irrelevant. However the business was undergoing a substantial refinancing and Robert's lack of attention to detail almost killed the deal. He was dismissed for what he failed to do – not rewarded for his successes.

Getting things done

Think about the tasks that you have facing you and write down the three things that you dislike, avoid or simply do hastily or badly. Ask yourself the following questions

'What is important about this task?'
'What is important to other people about this task?'
'How important is it to my career that I accomplish this task?'

Failure to tackle them will bring consequences. You will damage your reputation in either a small or a major way and these things accumulate. You do not wish to be known as the one who is always missing deadlines or never finishing something off.

Useful tactics

Whatever strategy you have developed to avoid doing the things you don't like, let's analyse how you do it. At the moment your strategy consistently produces a predictable outcome that is sabotaging your other well formed strategies to get on well in work. Your strategy is a problem for you and when you have a problem you are not in charge of your life but you are at effect – you are out of control and at the mercy of events.

The reasons for this could be that your starting point is feeling overwhelmed by the magnitude of the task. The only way forward is to break the task down into manageable chunks and get down to the detail. This will be achieved by hunting down the detail and the question 'How specifically ...?' will allow you to identify the individual elements.

Another reason is that perhaps you are not sufficiently motivated to do the task so reframing your thinking will help you change your motivation into a positive stream of energy.

Take an example of what you do badly. It might be something simple like getting your expenses in on time, something that will cause you cash flow problems, will mean your department can't put together a proper set of accounts and it will leave a number of people with an unclear set of numbers.

Step outside the problem and look at yourself. Ask yourself 'How do I do that?' Keep asking the question until you have loosened all of the edges of such an unhelpful strategy. You will come up with the exact pattern of behaviour that you use to make sure you don't do your expenses. Once you have worked it out, it may look like this:

- I am busy doing other things
- I push all the receipts in pockets, wallets, computer bag, drawers
- I can't find them when I need them
- I find lots of other things to do
- The deadline creeps up on me
- I am out of the office and can't do it

Look at the strategy that you have just elicited and look at the sequence that it happens in. Is it absolutely accurate?

Now ask yourself the question 'Can you remember a time when you did get work in on time?' and recall all of the memories of that event. Make sure that memory is intense.

Holding the memories of your successful strategy clearly in your head, now look at the stage of your unwanted strategy and decide to install new elements. This change will bring about sufficient changes so that you will have installed a new strategy that produces the desired outcome – expenses submitted on time. Check with yourself that this would work and ask yourself 'What is the problem I thought I had with expenses?'

Looking the part

Energetic people tend to have the kind of physiology, tonality and language of energetic people. How can you use all of these to work for you so that not only are you an energetic person, you look it and sound it too?

Physiology

Think about how you sit when you are in the office, in a meeting or sitting in front of a customer. In order to show that you are alert, full of get up and go and bristling with the vitality needed to get the job done, make sure that you sit up straight and you do not slouch. You could even discipline yourself to sit so that your back does not touch the chair, forcing you into a state of alertness. You will not slump in the chair or lounge in it. You won't have your hands behind your head with your chair pushed back from the table. You will be the epitome of the alert and busy worker. Look at your team. How are they behaving? You can either intervene directly and tell them to adopt a positive stance or if you are too late and you find yourself watching them give the wrong impression in a meeting, you can intervene by establishing close rapport with them, matching their body language, their breathing and their eye movements. Make gradual changes so that you are sitting in the right way and you will by subtle pacing and leading have brought them to the right position. See Chapter 8 on Communication to see how you do this. Remember that Energy is not just about you – it is about those around you.

Tonality

You may be someone who naturally speaks in a tone that is quite loud, assertive and strong. If you are not, there will be occasions when you may decide to adopt it. If you are naturally soft spoken or if you speak slowly, choose the times when you will increase the volume and increase the pace. Think of someone you know who is renowned for their energy. Think of their tones in a meeting and decide to match them.

Language

Consider your vocabulary and start to adopt a language pattern that is vibrant. Words such as:

Fast
Moving
Pace
Deadline
Go
Now
Immediate

Lost something?

Have you ever been in a situation when you were about to go out of the door for an important meeting and suddenly you realize that you can't find something vital – a file, a 'phone, car keys, a memory stick. Time is against you and your instinctive reaction may be to launch into panic mode. You scrabble round your desk, you search your pockets, you throw out the contents of your computer bag and the scene is looking chaotic. The chances of finding the lost article are reducing by the minute. Remember in this situation that sometimes inaction is in itself a vital form of action. The next time you misplace something, for it is not lost, it is merely in a place where you put it and you at the moment cannot recall exactly where that is, do this:

Stop. Think. Clear your mind with the windscreen wiper that breaks state as this current panic mode is not conducive to solution finding. Think back to the last time that you had the lost article. Flip through your memory bank and think of that occasion. Step into that picture of yourself holding in your hand the item you are now looking for. In your mind's eye look around you and remember just where you are and what you are doing. Be there now. Holding the item in your hand, ask yourself 'What do I need to know now in order to find it?' You will discover that this calm and controlled way of searching will bring you the results you need. Your days of frantic searches are officially over and your energy is now saved for use elsewhere.

Car parking

In *The Book of Luck – Brilliant ideas for creating your own success and making life go your way*, a book that Heather

Summers and I wrote together, we urged people strongly to use the power of the mind to park their car. How many times have you driven round, desperately hunting for a parking place, knowing you are running out of time and needing to have your car parked so you can get on your way? Bringing this under your control will reduce stress in your life and allow you to focus on what is more important.

The next time you are going out in your car, as you get behind the steering wheel, think of where you plan to park. Be very clear, very specific and know the exact spot. Is it outside a particular shop? What is the name of the street? See it clearly in your mind's eye. Is it a nice comfortably large spot that you just drive into or is one where you will demonstrate your parallel parking skills? See the space and now see yourself arriving and parking successfully. Get out of the car, get the parking ticket on it, lock it and walk away.

Now that you have safely parked, you can start the journey in real time, knowing that your car parking spot awaits.

> Remember: however much you are doing, by tapping into the universe of energy and using the anchor of determined self-belief, you will exceed all expectations.

Curiosity

HOW TO FIND OUT WHAT YOU DON'T KNOW

"The map is not the territory"

How many times have you heard people say that a business that stands still is slipping backwards? Change is the norm and successful businesses are ones which are always one step ahead. While their competitors are reverse engineering their products, they are pioneering new products, new ideas and new ways of doing things. Henry Ford once said that if he had asked his customers what they wanted, they would have said that they wanted a faster horse.

New ideas in a business provide the energy and fuel of the business, giving it the momentum it needs to continue to operate successfully in today's challenging markets. One of the great presuppositions of NLP is that 'The Map is not the Territory.' I interpret this as an encouragement to recognize that although you believe you have a clear definition of where you are, what you do and how you behave, there is more to life than this, no matter how much you love what you have. There is always more and the unknown will always be greater than the known. How do you access this? Via curiosity. Let's start the hunt therefore for the territory.

David Apicella, European Human Resources Director of MWV, puts curiosity right at the top of the list of attributes of high performers in business. He said:

'I believe the best performers are people who just enjoy learning; they are inquisitive and want to feel that they can make a difference to an organization, whether this difference is small or large. This can be quite often obvious from the day you select them and often this desire to learn is also demonstrated in their personal lives outside the working environment. This could range from learning new sporting activities, through to learning musical instruments. It could also be demonstrated in other ways, maybe in the community, social clubs, teams, church, family or friends. These people are busy and enjoy being just that.

When selecting the correct people, despite the obvious technical or professional attributes essential to do the role, I look for an enthusiasm to learn and the desire to improve themselves as they are core traits that should not be ignored. These people are quite often ambitious and want to succeed. However their status or hierarchy in an organization is not their main driving factor. They really just want to learn, contribute and be recognized.'

I have a client, the chairman and owner of a very successful and profitable business, who likes to spend more time out of the office than he spends in it. He travels the world attending exhibitions, visiting suppliers, talking to customers and being curious to find out what he doesn't know. He returns to his business revitalized, full of enthusiasm and full of ideas about how he can do things differently. His business is constantly reinventing itself and it is going from strength to strength. In contrast, in the mid '90s I worked with a client who was a knit wear manufacturer in Scotland. The business had been going for many years, supplying the main high street multiples. He was obsessed with his business but rarely left the office, sticking to tried and tested ways. Because he could not envisage a time when the knitting looms would not be running in Scotland, he assumed that customers would not be attracted by cheap imports from Asia. Sadly, the world changed around him, cost became more important than quality and Chinese manufacturers were absorbing change and difference so their quality improved. Business fell away sharply and eventually his business closed.

The best business is one that is constantly looking outside to see what is going on. It stands to reason, therefore, that the best business is one that has people inside it who are open to new opportunities and who are actively seeking them out. Because you are going to move from good to great in your performance at work, how do you make sure that your feet are not stuck in the present and you are actively scanning the horizon for new ideas? As John A. Shedd said, 'A ship in harbour is safe – but that is not what ships are built for.'

There are some people who are naturally inclined towards change and to new ways of doing things. Google offer their engineers '20-percent time' so that they are free to work on what they are really passionate about. They believe that this opportunity to explore unknown paths and to satisfy their curiosity has brought about the development of AdSense for Content and Orkut. Sir James Dyson, the brilliant inventor and entrepreneur, said 'I love making mistakes. People who make the most mistakes should get the most marks because they ventured out and discovered things.'

In order to become like them or to convince yourself that you could be fired up by allowing your curiosity to flow, consider what the curiosity options look like by filling in the chart below. Designed according to NLP's Cartesian coordinates, it is a favourite way of mine to expand boundaries and to realize the consequences of action or inaction. You might like to think about impact on the business, on customers, on profitability, on personal development, on potential redundancies, enhanced profits, increased budgets for training and development. Just a few ideas to stimulate thought!

What wouldn't happen if you were curious and you were the spirited advocate of change, bringing new ideas to the table? What won't happen if you are curious? 1. 2. 3. 4. 5. 6. 7. 8. 9. 10.	What would happen if you were curious and you were the spirited advocate of change, bringing new ideas to the table? What will happen if you are curious? 1. 2. 3. 4. 5. 6. 7. 8. 9. 10.
What wouldn't happen if you were not curious and you were not the spirited advocate of change and if you did not bring new ideas to the table? What won't happen if you are not curious? 1. 2. 3. 4. 5. 6. 7. 8. 9. 10.	What would happen if you were not curious and you were not the spirited advocate of change and if you did not bring new ideas to the table? What will happen if you are not curious? 1. 2. 3. 4. 5. 6. 7. 8. 9. 10.

It would seem, therefore, that most people will acknowledge that curiosity could add value to individuals, team and companies. A disinterest in life outside your confines where you do not know or care what your colleagues or competitors are doing could damage you and could damage your business. You may already be very skilled in exploration of new ideas and you may already be the hottest innovator in town. If you are not, do you know someone who is? If it does not come to you naturally, now is the time to model excellence.

How not to do it

A service business was going through a period of tremendous change. They were facing tougher markets with an expectation from customers that they were in a cost down environment. All the staff wanted increased salaries and benefits and the only way it could be achieved was through better processes, better systems and using all available technology to maximize revenue. Peter was a key member of the team but he was totally disinterested in any of the innovations. He wanted to do things his way, the old way and would not even listen to potential advantages that would be brought. He refused to use the custom-built software system that was designed to improve billing systems, he would not use the shared resources and processes and was the only person to stick to the old ways that he knew. He was dismissive of computers, e-mails and software applications and because he did not want to find out what it was all about, he deliberately put himself outside the mainstream of the business.

No one could persuade him to explore the possibilities of the new and the different and the result for the company was that they suffered the frustrations of incomplete information at every level. Despite the value that Peter brought to the business in many other ways, this out of date attitude that sprang out of his lack of curiosity was his undoing and after numerous warnings, he was eventually dismissed and he didn't have a clue how to get another job. The world had moved on and left him behind.

Modelling excellence

One way that businesses measure their success is to look at what competitors are doing and seeing how they are getting there. If they are using processes or branding or techniques that look interesting and effective, these innovations are copied or amended in some way to bring about change. The Japanese manufacturing methods were hugely in vogue in Europe and their ways became part of the common parlance of manufacturing vocabulary. Businesses were modelling what they saw as excellence.

Successful people are often asked if they have a role model and usually they cite a close family member and an inspirational figure from the past or the present. We look at others and admire them for what they do and how they do it and we seek to imitate those qualities and take them for our own. How do we do this? We pay attention to what they say and how they say it. We look closely at how they behave in meetings and in negotiations. We listen to how they phrase things and the more tuned in we are to what makes them the person they are, the more likely we are to be able to use them as a model of excellence and use them as our own personal touchstone of excellence. We aspire to be like them and therefore get the same results that they do. Imitation is the sincerest form of flattery and this skill in noticing carefully the skills of others and then turning them into a process to help you and your colleagues will help you along the path from good to great.

Who are your role models?

Take the time to think of three people that you believe were the greatest inventors, explorers or risk takers of all time. They may be current business people like James Dyson, Richard Branson or Tim Smit. They may be 'celebrity' people like Simon Cowell, David Beckham or Peter Andre who have used what they have got to create a profile and a personal brand. Equally they could be people from history who have altered the course of life because of what they have done, people like Mahatma Gandhi, Nelson Mandela, Captain Cook or James Logie Baird. Think of three people you know, either people you have worked with, people you have studied with or relatives. Make sure that these people are ones who do the unexpected, have shown a curiosity that led them to paths outside the norm. Then select one from each group and decide that you are going to model this pattern of excellence. The best way of improving who you are and what you do is to find someone who does things well. In this instance, we are looking for someone with that joyful curiosity that is followed through and results delivered. It is not necessarily someone who excels in every other sphere. They might be a terrible team player or not be able to make decisions. This we will ignore. We want to look at how they use curiosity to bring an added dimension to their work.

First of all, look at the unattainable person you have selected, the historical person, the high profile business person or the celebrity. You can't speak to them personally but there is enough information about them for you to find out what they do and how they do it. Use spare time to research them on the Internet, perhaps in your lunch hours or during a quiet night in. What is it that they do that is radical and different? Find out how they do it, why it is important to them and what skills do they have to get there.

Now let's look at the person you know. Using all of your well developed skills in developing rapport, find the chance to talk to them about their skills in curiosity. Decide that you are going to use the opportunity to question them closely about those skills. You may be able to get all of the information that you need in one meeting but you may need to see them several times. If you have to make contact via the telephone, make sure you use all of your telephonic rapport building skills. Use your voice to match theirs, using the same tone, the same pace and the same volume. Listen to their language and be sure to tune into whatever system of thinking they prefer. Don't tell a visual person that you can hear them and don't tell an auditory person that you can see what they mean.

Focusing just on their curiosity, ask them to imagine them- selves at a time when they were curious. Now put to them a number of questions, all in the present tense. Your goal is to find out how they do what they do. Questions might therefore be along the lines of:

◆ What are you thinking when you are being curious?
◆ How exactly do you uncover new possibilities?

♦ How do you connect with all of these new things?
♦ What do you say to yourself when you are doing it?
♦ What is important to you?
♦ For what purpose do you do this?
♦ How specifically do you do it?
♦ What happens when you get it?
♦ What do you believe about yourself?

Take careful notes and work out what their strategy is. Now you can use their curiosity strategy for your own ends. You can convert it into a simple strategy that will work for you and that you can assimilate into the way that you work.

Within the structure of one of my clients, a UK PLC, was Mike, a Divisional Finance Director who aspired to greater things. He was financially very strong and he was a good manager of his people. His boss had reservations about his ability to add value at a higher level and so he put Mike through a series of psychometric aptitude tests. The results for the verbal reasoning were abysmal. He scored a 3 percentile ranking, meaning that his skills in expressing himself and articulating opinions and views were likely to be much poorer than most of the management population. When questioned, Mike said that he never ever read anything, not the morning paper, not a book, nothing. He worked and then he watched television but he did not read. As a result, his intellectual growth had stultified. He had limited abilities to express himself both verbally and in writing. He had not developed and grown and it was decided that he did not have the breadth of knowledge to move to a higher level. His career never picked up from that as he accepted that this was the way that he was.

Being open to new technologies

Another plan could be to recognize that the digital world we are living in needs people to be alert to new technologies and to be aware of the possible benefits of social media. I am not talking about using Facebook to exchange social chat. I am talking about the serious use and changing use of social media to bring about change in business practice. There is no room in today's fast paced world for the business dinosaur.

Let's look at LinkedIn for example, www.linkedin.com, the best site for professional exchanges. It is a global website where professionals make contact with each other, form special interest groups and link together to add value. If you don't know anything about it, get online now and have a look. Find the company or the individual that seem to use LinkedIn to best effect and ask yourself the questions that will allow you to define a strategy for your own use. Model the best and you will find a short cut that will work for you. Modelling excellence is all about being curious about what makes other people so good at what they do.

Twitter is a global social networking site where messages ('tweets') are no longer than 140 characters and are sent out to 'followers'. Sarah Brown and Demi Moore are keen Twitterers and people use it for a number of reasons. Growing a huge number of followers means that your messages are being sent to a wide audience and by following huge numbers yourself, you gain an insight into the world of others. It is used to share information, seek help and support and is increasingly being seen as a way to grow brands and businesses. Innocent Drinks use it to show their quirky different style and marketing departments are becoming increasingly aware of Twitter power. There are those who deride it and those who are obsessed with it. In order to find out where you sit and to have an informed view, make up your mind to explore it (www. twitter.com). Unleash your curiosity and see what goes on. There are no boundaries on Twitter just as there are no boundaries in life. Find the Twitter business experts and see how they do it. Experiment in an anonymous way to see how it might or might not help you. Curiosity does not necessarily result in a positive outcome but it will show your boss and your colleagues that you are alert and open to what is around. You yourself will become a role model as your team members see that you are constantly bringing new ideas and plans to the table. Be known as an early adopter of technology as this is the best way to show your wish to be open to new ideas.

Curiosity and other people

When you are sitting next to someone on a bus or a train, do you listen to your music, read your book, sleep? Do you wonder about the people around you and allow yourself to surmise what their lives look like? Start to develop a sense of curiosity in small ways and then allow them to grow. Inventions, creations, life saving therapies grew out of a sense of curiosity.

Clare Howard of Academy 28 says:

'The old rules said that "Curiosity killed the cat. Satisfaction brought it back." In today's world, satisfaction leads to arrogant and smug fat cats; whereas curiosity is the lifeblood of organizations and individuals. As well as keeping you humble, it keeps you on your toes, alert and alive, ready to take risks and to seize opportunities others don't even realize are there.'

Test yourself

Now that you have decided to increase your awareness of what might have previously passed you by, train yourself and test yourself in simple ways. Think of a meeting you had in the last ten days. Recall who was there, what they wore, where they sat and exactly what they looked like. What colour are their eyes? Every time you do this you will bring greater detail and greater clarity to your recollections. It is not because your memory is getting better, it is because your powers of observation are improving. The more you notice, the more inspiration you will get.

Observing other people

Body language is not just spotting when someone folds their arms and then leaping to the conclusion that they are becoming defensive. Noticing the changes in other people is probably much more subtle and these minute changes that keep on happening are sending meaningful messages to those who are interested. Changes in emotions are reflected in skin tone, the tone of muscles, breathing rate and where it is coming from, lower lip size and the eye focus.

This chart is for you to store in your head, not to whip out at the next management or sales meeting to take notes on the participants. Log it in your head so the next time you need to, you can access it by moving your eyes up to the right and hey presto, it will be there.

Muscle tone
Tight..Relaxed
Breathing rate
Fast..slow
Depth of breathing (shallow or deep)
High...low
Personal engagement
Tuned in...switched off
Eye focus
Sharp...defocused
Pupil dilation
Dilated...not dilated

We all notice when someone blushes or goes scarlet or pale. Truly curious people can see the slight nuances of change and detect the impact of what they are saying and doing. This gives the versatility to adjust the tone of your message accordingly. Keep asking yourself the question 'How is this person reacting to what I am saying?' and you will be more finely tuned into the universe.

Habits

The enemy of curiosity is habit. We are all creatures of habit and we have routines and rituals that make our lives comfortable. People who are comfortable in being uncomfortable are those who put themselves in situations where they don't know what is going to happen. As soon as you are away from the familiar, anything can happen. I am not suggesting that you start training to row the Atlantic rather than catch a plane. Start by breaking small habits and bring about change in your life. For example, you could try to:

1. Read a different newspaper
2. Go to work a different way
3. Eat in a different place
4. Cook a different meal
5. Listen to a different radio station
6. Accept an invitation you would normally decline
7. Talk to the person you normally avoid
8. Work in a different part of the office
9. Visit a different website every day
10. Add five people to your www.linkedin.com network every week
11. Read a book every week
12. Read a different specialist magazine every week

Curiosity will give you the additional information and insights that fuel new ideas. Every boss wants to see team members who are innovative and adding value. By making sure that you have an external focus you will bring new perspectives. If you notice more things that are going on, you will have insights that others lack. By attending events that extend your network of connections, you will have more resources than others.

Curiosity and learning

Gareth James of People Plus says:

'You don't know everything. You'll never know everything. It's OK not to know. Ask. Research. Learn.'

Remember: the map is not the territory so there is significantly more to learn, more to see and more to give than you can ever have at the moment.

Communication

HOW TO BECOME THE BEST COMMUNICATOR YOU KNOW

"We are always communicating and the meaning of the communciation is the response you receive"

Communication cuts across every day of our lives and the technologies that we live with in the 21st century mean that there are greater expectations of our engagement. There is rarely a chance to slip off the radar and be out of touch. Texting, e-mailing, telephone calls, social media such as Facebook and Twitter, they are all pushing us down a road of constant interaction with others. The benefit is that we are always in touch and potentially in control of our jobs. The downside is that communicating the wrong message in the wrong way or the right message with the wrong tone can be counterproductive.

It is not enough to do a good job. You also have to be seen to be doing a good job and the only way that this will happen if you take charge of what you communicate and how you communicate it. What you think you are saying is not necessarily what someone hears. Listening is as important as talking and all of the elements of non-verbal communication can be sending strong messages to help you. All you have to do is to notice them, incorporate them into your actions and decisions and you are on the route to success.

Imagine your boss tells you that you will be expected to attend a meeting tomorrow morning at 8am and your response is 'Great'. If said with a smile and enthusiasm, it means you are pleased. If you raise your eyes to heaven and mutter it under your breath, you are in fact conveying the opposite. The subtleties of communication move far beyond the words that you use.

The best communicators are those who have a deep understanding of the people they are working with. They are aware of what can go wrong and they actively work to address it. However good you are at communicating, take this opportunity to look at how you do it from a different perspective. In the course of this chapter you will find new signposts that will point you to the shortest route to the most effective methods of communication.

The Structure of Communication

Communication is much more than language. A 1996 study by Professor Albert Mehrabin of the University of California entitled 'Silent Messages' showed that what you say has significantly less impact than how you say it and what you look like when you are saying it.

Verbal	7%
Tonality	38%
Physiology	55%

Simply put, the meaning of the language you are using can be altered by your demeanour, your tone of voice, the pitch of your voice and the silent messages you are sending along with the words. If you are agreeing to do something and feel uncertain about your ability to do it on time, just saying the words 'Of course I can' will probably not convey confidence and enthusiasm. Your emotions will be on display in subtle ways and will undermine the vocabulary. In order to be in charge of your own mind, discover what messages you are sending other people that are distorting the pattern of communication.

Meaningful communication requires effort and persistence and, based on solid rapport, will bring about immediate results. The joy of NLP is that it is not a three year program. The impact is immediate and can be measured.

Establishing Rapport – The starting point of excellent communication

As we saw in Chapter 4, the starting point of any connection with someone else, whoever it is, has got to be building a rapport with them. Let's look at building rapport. The purpose of it is to bypass the conscious mind and to get in touch with the unconscious mind and to gain uncritical acceptance.

Whatever you are doing, it has got to be so much simpler if you get on well with the people you are dealing with. You don't have to like them or to want to be their best friend. What you need to do is to find a common understanding that will allow you to work well together. Sometimes it comes naturally and what we want to do now is to work out what happens when you do it naturally and translate that into different situations. If you are the active person who takes responsibility for making sure that the relationship is working well, then you will be in charge. Being in charge gives you control and suddenly life looks different.

In order to be in rapport with someone, it is not actually necessary to like them. Working well with people is based on more than just liking people. It is about respect, trust and acceptance of difference. Working hard to create rapport will increase the chances of mutual respect being established and this is a solid foundation for an excellent working relationship.

In my role as a headhunter, I had a meeting with Olivia in London and we were there to discuss a potential joint venture. I was disconcerted to find that she was quite clearly matching and mirroring whatever I did, carefully speaking at the same pace as I did and using the same tone. She questioned me carefully to identify areas of common ground. She asked me about my family and my interests and declared where we were similar. After 15 minutes she clapped her hands and said 'Right. Now we have got that rapport stuff over, let's get down to the real business'.

I found out later that she had been on a one day NLP course and had decided to seize upon rapport building as a useful

technique. She had failed to incorporate it into her natural style and to integrate it in the whole process so the result was not quite what she expected.
You won't be surprised to hear that there was no joint venture.

Creating rapport to facilitate better communication

The basis of strong relationships is founded on a sense of rapport. Being in tune, at ease and feeling linked in an important way with your colleagues and the values of your organization is the foundation for excellent relationships with colleagues and managers. The basic ingredients for fitting in, getting on and enjoying significant common ground with your colleagues are probably already there as you have chosen to work in your current environment. Something attracted you in the first place so the way to increase success and to make a greater impact is by gaining the value of deeper levels of rapport with more people. What NLP teaches is the technique to grow rapport and develop it actively by choosing to go the extra mile by yourself.

The first step

If you watch friends when they are chatting together with the ease of a comfortable relationship, you will see that they probably are behaving in the same way. They sit in the same way, they have the same mannerisms, the same pitch of voice and probably even the same tone. They are unconsciously matching and mirroring each other. They are probably even using the same kind of language as each other. They are probably in deep rapport without even knowing it is happening. They are chatting away freely in an environment of trust and openness. How useful would this talent be for you in meetings with customers or colleagues?

In one of my headhunting assignments I was interviewing Engineering Directors for a whole day in Glasgow. Part of the skill set I was looking for was an excellent communicator as the job involved managing a big team and talking to customers. Bill came into the room and he carefully positioned his chair so he would not have to look at me. He gazed out of the window for the whole time and could not bring himself to behave as though there was anyone else in the room. He scored zero rapport points and did not get the job.

By bringing rapport building to a conscious level and deciding that this is going to be the starting point for you with everyone you meet, you will be adding value at every level. It must become natural and easy, something that will benefit both parties rather than it degenerating into some kind of party trick that will give you control in a relationship. To make it easier to get on with people, find areas of common interest. Find out if you worked in the same sectors, went to the same university, lived in the same town, travelled to the same region. The way you establish this is by questioning. Asking questions and replying by disclosing information of your own will help pave the way to greater rapport. Questioning, listening, making connections and responding with something of your own will be a standard part of your engagement with others.

The process of establishing rapport

1. Physiology

As physiology is considered to be 55% of the process of communication, let's start by understanding how to make sure that this is the core of everything you do with others. Begin by deciding if you plan to match or to mirror the person you are communicating with. Have a conscious awareness of what you plan to do. Matching is acting as if both of you have your right hand up and mirroring is as if one has the right hand up and the other person the left hand.

You are looking at:

♦ Posture
♦ Gesture
♦ Breathing
♦ Facial expression and blinking
♦ Breathing

It is critical that you keep this below the level of conscious awareness as otherwise it becomes intrusive, worrying and even quite spooky. You must be sure to stop it from becoming invasive. True physiological rapport will ensure that conversations you have will sound like an internal dialogue.

School uniform was devised to create a sense of belonging. By dressing the same, pupils already have something in common. In the workplace this too is important. If everyone in the business is wearing jeans and tee shirts, you will stand out if you are there in smart suits, shorts and ties or stylish skirts and stilettos. You may decide to do this as a deliberate ploy to be different and to stand out but this can make it harder to become part of the group. Look around you and then look in the mirror. Is there room for change?

Food and drink are also a potential area for mismatch. As a vegetarian of twenty years' standing, I have had to develop ways of avoiding the embarrassment of being in the wrong place and then unwittingly causing a minor fuss about food. Another client is a high energy group where they demolish vast quantities of red wine and stay out until four in the morning. Unless you have the staying power to match them, it is important to develop strategies to cope that leave you still in rapport with them and yet doing what you want.

I have learnt to scan the menu at the speed of light, find something that I can eat and just order it. This is in contrast to someone I met at conference who created a huge fuss about his wheat allergies, demanded rice cakes for breakfast and had the hosts running around in a state of embarrassment. Any established rapport was quickly eroded and the group never really recovered from the underlying message that the hospitality was not quite right.

The best strategy for being with a group who drink a lot is to have a glass of water at hand so you are seen to be constantly lifting a glass to your lips. The morning after the night before, a colleague commented admiringly on my astonishing drinking prowess. Rapport was strong, water was quaffed and my reputation was riding high!

A useful intervention

The next time you are in a meeting and someone is distinctly nervous because they have to make a presentation or need to do something in front of others, you will notice that their breathing is quicker because of this nervousness. Match this breathing and gradually slow it down. As you are in rapport in all of the other elements, the person will slow their breathing, become calmer and overcome the nerves that could have jeopardized their work.

The clicking pen

Have you ever been in a meeting with someone who is clicking their pen? As soon as you notice it seems to become louder and to drive you mad, affecting your concentration and therefore your performance. Telling them to put the pen away is not going to help you, particularly if it is your boss or a customer so make them stop in a wordless way. Ensuring that you keep it below the level of consciousness, as they click, you tap. Match them rhythmically and gradually slow it down until you stop – and so do they.

---

2. Voice Tonality
The areas of focus here are:

Tone – the pitch of the voice
Tempo – the speed of speech

Timbre – the quality of the voice
Volume – the loudness of the voice

Voice tonality is something that will become second nature to you. It will help you in face-to-face meetings and it will also be powerful in telephone conversations. It isn't necessary always to be physically present in order to be in rapport.

Listen carefully to tone, volume, depth and pitch. Use the same to reflect back to them who they are. When they hear this they will feel instant rapport and empathy. They will feel that they know you.

I worked with a Call Centre that needed to increase their sales dramatically. The business plan called for doubling the volume without increasing the number of staff. They decided to focus entirely on the voice and the language of their operatives and within three weeks they achieved their objectives. They asked their staff to be flexible in their language and never to use the same phrase twice. They were not even allowed to say 'My name is ... ,' twice. Instead they had to think of alternatives, such as 'I am calling from' or 'You don't know me but'. This became a game around the table and this freshness of approach was transmitted down the phone. The variety of language in the sales pitch made it more credible and therefore more effective.

All negative language was erased and staff excelled at saying 'I prefer' rather than 'I don't like'.

The focus of the business was on skilful language rather than volume of calls and it paid off.

3. Words

The final 7% of communication consists of the words that we use and these can be summarized as:

♦ Verbs
♦ Key words
♦ Common experiences and associations
♦ Content chunks

One of the toughest jobs a sales person has to do is to write proposals or tenders. The ones most likely to be successful are those that reflect the language patterns and vocabulary of the decision maker. In order to make this work for you, when you are engaged in the preliminary discussions about the piece of work you are going to be pitching for, write down phrases and words that are being used. Notice if they are short sentences or long ones and use these exact words and language patterns in your proposal. They will have resonance and you will sound familiar – a good start!

Pacing and Leading

Once you believe you have made steps towards the right levels of rapport, you can then subtly change the scenario to draw people further into your state. This is achieved by pacing and leading. Pacing involves 'matching' someone for a while, which means going at their pace. You are following them until you have gained sufficient rapport to allow you to start to change what you are doing. Now you are leading and the individual will follow. The success of pacing and leading relies on the quality of rapport that you have build up. If you go too fast or move too abruptly you will break rapport in which case you will have to go right back to the beginning and start again. The formula for pacing and leading is:

♦ Pace, pace, pace, lead
♦ Pace, pace, lead, lead
♦ Pace, lead, lead, lead

and repeating this pattern until the desired state is achieved.

The joys of great rapport

How will you know when you haven't got the right levels of rapport? Simple! You will feel slightly ill at ease, you can't quite find the right connection, and you may occasionally struggle to find the right words. You may maintain a business like communication but humour, banter and personal confidence that are the food of growing relationships are absent. The consequence for you in business terms is that you are not influencing decisions, plans, projects, quotes or people in the way that you would like and people do not necessarily listen to you in the way that you would prefer. Equally, you may feel that colleagues exclude you or leave you slightly on the margins of conversations and groups. If you are out of rapport with someone, it is easier to become irritated by foibles, you will be more likely to overreact to problems and issues and you will be less likely to give the benefit of the doubt. People who are not in synch with you may react in the same way as well. The atmosphere is one that can be slightly tense and will drain energy in negative way. So what can you do to develop better rapport, greater influence, clearer communication and to establish trust?

Walking into a room

How many times have you had to walk into a room and wonder how you are going to get on? You could be visiting customers, cold calling, making a presentation to the board or meeting colleagues in the business that you haven't worked with before. The only contact you will have had will have been by e-mail or telephone and this is the first occasion when you are face to face. Success will come to you if you create excellent impressions wherever you go. It is easy if you are meeting people who share your personal style or knowledge base but can be more challenging when you have yet to establish any common ground.

Using difference constructively

Remember that business often thrives on the adrenalin of debate, opposing views and energetic conversation.

What would you do if you worked in a harmonious organization where all meetings were constructive, courteous and calm? This might not be what you always want so you might choose purposefully to inject some energy into the meetings by challenging the harmony. How could you do this? Break rapport: Change your tone, the speed of your speech, lean back in your chair and mismatch.

Are you listening?

Everyone seems to be looking for 'good communicators' and yet people seem to have different definitions of what that can mean. A good communicator is someone who is listened to and who gets their point across. Failure to achieve this means that the business is not getting the valuable input it requires and individuals are frustrated as they feel that they are not giving of their best and they are being ignored. How many times have you been in a meeting where you have been dying to say something but you can't get a word in edgeways? Also, how many times have you been sitting in a meeting working out what you are going to say next rather than listening to the person who is speaking? Communication is speaking, it is listening and it is body language. The non verbal stuff makes just as much impact as the verbal. Attentive listening as well as appropriate contributions make for great relationships. Sometimes silence is more powerful than words and the best way of making sure that what you are doing is the most appropriate is by ensuring that you are in tune with the meeting, in tune with the objectives and in tune with the individuals. I recently visited an organization to work with key individuals in the management team. Every single one complained about the poor communication in the organization, believing it to be something that 'happened' and was the responsibility of others. I sent a long personal e-mail to each of them, raising particular issues and asking them what they thought. Not a single one replied so the meaning I received from their non-communication to me was that they couldn't be bothered.

Influencing and persuasion

The most effective person in the organization is the one who can use their skills to influence others, win their trust and then persuade them to adopt their thinking.

An enterprising Sales Manager needed to grow his sales line by creating an in house Call Centre and needed to recruit people for this role that needed tenacious and outstanding sales people. He drafted an advertisement and put it online and was amazed when he received not a single reply. The advert read like this: 'Wanted – cold calling machines. We need to get results from you and to see you hitting 90 calls a day. Please send your CV to …'

What happens, therefore, if you decide that a certain course of action, for example developing a new range of products, changing suppliers, reorganising the team, would be the best thing for the business? You may well have ample evidence to back up your plans yet you cannot bring anyone round to your mindset. You look around and you believe that you have established deep rapport. You have been sure to incorporate all of the VAK and AD language so that you have tapped into all of these preferred systems but you are still getting nowhere. What else can NLP give you that will show you how to increase your talents in persuasion?

Negotiating and countering arguments against

The art of negotiating is one that can be fraught with difficulties. If you are in sales you will be measured by results and your focus will be on achieving those targets. In order to make every sales meeting count, you need to be sure that your negotiations skills are finely tuned and destined for success.

Whatever you are negotiating for, wouldn't you prefer to go into it knowing you were going to get what you want? Think of situations when improved negotiation skills would assist you:

♦ Winning the sale
♦ Winning the argument
♦ Getting promoted
♦ Getting an increase in your budget
♦ Adding people to your team
♦ Increasing your sales territory
♦ Persuading your boss to give you the day off

In tune – Listen, look and learn

Learning to read eye movements

Here is where NLP comes into its own and presents you with a simple yet effective way of working out what people are thinking. Picture how useful this will be when you are in front of a customer, gauging how they are responding to what you are telling them. It isn't mind reading, it isn't hocus pocus, it is just following a logical pattern to work out how someone is gaining their information. Let me put this in the simplest way possible. Then you must take it and use it and practice it so that it becomes second nature to you to look people straight in the eyes when they are talking to you so you get into the habit of working out how they are thinking. This is itself is a first class way of building up rapport so you will be achieving two things with one stratagem.

Let's test your power of observation first. What colour eyes does your boss have? If you know the answer, well done. If you don't, then from now on, set yourself the challenge of making eye contact with people that you meet. Test yourself after any meeting and recall the colour of people's eyes. Some people do it naturally. Practice it enough and you will become one of those people. The ability to observe detail is what separates the good from the great so add the eye reading knowledge to your skill set and then use it.

The eyes are indicators of the way you are thinking so by watching how people move their eyes, you will be increasing your communication skills. First of all, find a compliant friend and experiment a little.

Look your friend in the eyes and ask them to spell 'extraordinary.' Watch carefully as you are looking for movements that might be fleeting and hard to detect. In order to make the movements more pronounced, you could try asking them to spell the word backwards, a challenge even for the best of spellers. They will typically look up and move their eyes to the left or right. They are recalling information and it is as if they are reading it from a book or a whiteboard.

Now test your friend by asking them to remember the voice of their mother or their favourite song. Their eyes will move sideways to the left.

Of course, all this will be inverted in some people, particularly if they are left handed so before you make assumptions about their thought processes, check with a spelling question.

Eye movement summary

1. Imagined images that are created and not existing.
    Eyes up and to the right
2. Remembering images from the past, such as the house you lived in, where you went for your birthday dinner.
    Eyes up and to the left

3. Constructing sounds that are in conflict with reality, such as a colleague speaking like Bart Simpson.
    Eyes move to the side and to the right

4. Remembering a familiar sound such as the kettle boiling, the water cooler emptying.
    Eyes move to the side and to the left

5. Recollecting feeling and emotions, such as anger, sadness, joy, triumph.
    Eyes move down and to the right

6. Talking to yourself, the internal dialogue that gives you the energy and motivation to do things.
    Eyes move down and to the left

7. Remembering things you have seen or things you are creating in your head.
    Eyes defocused and staring straight ahead

These clues to people's mental processes will give you the opportunity to alter how you deal with them. If people are accessing information by looking up and left or recalling what something looks like by staring straight ahead, allow them the time to gather the information to respond to you. Understanding how people marshal their thoughts and information will allow you to give them the scope that they need to be successful. Use this skill by allowing others to excel and enhance the results of the team.

The careful use of language

By crafting your language more carefully, you will create deeper rapport, increase understanding and get your colleagues on board with your ideas and decisions. You will create an environment of trust and confidence – all through rethinking how you use your words. Although language is less than 10% of overall communication, it is a vital 10%, particularly when you are in meetings, on the telephone or sending e-mails, texts and letters.

Sending the message that you mean

Here are that are key ways and three potential minefields when sending or receiving messages; definitely areas to be aware of and to avoid when you are aiming for success. These are things that we all do so the trick is to be aware not just of what you do but what others might be doing when they are talking to you.

1. Deletion

Confusion can arise in communication when some of the meaning is missing. By deleting some of the words, part of the connection with others is eroded or undermined. This isn't deliberate or malicious; it is just a way of ducking what is really going on.

For example, if you say 'Meetings in this organization are always a waste of time' or 'Manufacturing never get things out on time', there is a sub text that is unspoken that arouses suspicion. In order to be a team player who is clear and unambiguous, challenge statements like that with precise questioning such as

> 'Which meetings specifically?'
> 'What specifically is the issue on which we waste time?'
> 'Who in manufacturing is slowing the process down?'
> 'Where exactly is the bottle neck that is causing the delay?'

By confronting this kind of statement where there has been a deliberate or unconscious attempt to confuse what the real issue is you will drill down to the specifics, thus flushing out the true intention of the communication. Ensure that you do it in a way that is constructive and non threatening. This clarity in language will encourage people to say what they are thinking rather than holding back on a potentially useful contribution.

2. Generalizations

Generalizations are another unhelpful way of avoiding tackling issues and not facing facts. A popular one that I encounter in every business I go into is 'Communication is an issue across this business.' Another favourite is that 'Decision making is hopeless around here.' You will see that what would be a verb – communicating and deciding – has been changed into a noun. All of the energy has been taken out of the sentence so the shift of responsibility has gone from the individual to the corporate. Is the true meaning 'No one tells me what is going on' or 'I am not allowed to make decisions?'

In order to get back into control, it is time to ask yourself the question 'Who specifically is not talking to me in the way I want? How would I like the communication to change?' Great people are in control of life and what happens to generalizations means that there is something you cannot do. Challenge this by asking who is doing what and how they are doing it.

3. Distortions

Distortions in language occur either in the way things are said or the way that they are received. These occur in a number of ways and can radically alter the dynamics in a group. For example, a distortion occurs if someone says 'I know you don't like me' or 'I know he doesn't trust me' or 'You don't think I can do it.'

To check if these have any basis in reality, the question to ask 'How do you know ...?' By asking the question until you get right to the source of this information, you will uncover the truth rather than their perception. If you catch yourself using this kind of reading that is not based on any tangible evidence, then it is time to pull back and work out how you know that and what you mean by it. Getting to the source of this feeling will allow you to reappraise the data and your feelings about it.

Another distortion occurs when you hear someone saying 'You make me ...' For example 'You make me feel useless' or 'She makes me feel inadequate' or 'He makes me feel miserable'. Accepting (as we do) that you are in charge of yourself, then it follows that no one has the power to make you feel anything. You can, however, choose to feel like that.

The response to 'You make me feel miserable' is 'How does what I am doing cause you to choose to feel miserable?' Or alternatively 'How specifically do you feel miserable?'

Another kind of distortion that can step in the way of establishing good relationships with colleagues is deriving an outcome from a completely separate event. Let me explain. If your boss shouts at you for being late for work, you may say 'My boss is always shouting at me and does not like me.' Or, if you write a proposal that is rejected by your boss 'My proposal was rejected and my boss thinks my work is hopeless.'

This kind of connection from one event to deriving a separate meaning can be countered by challenging the assumption that lies at the heart. It could be done by saying:

'Have you ever shouted at someone that you liked?' or
'Have you ever criticized a piece of work and still valued the rest of that person's output?' or
How does your boss shouting mean that he does not like you?'

Deletions, distortions and generalizations are the filters in communication that can cause communication to get lost in transit. The solution is to have heightened awareness of what is going on and then to use the appropriate challenge to regain the clarity that is need in an organization to ensure that everyone is heading towards the same goal.

Powerful but fast – here's a tip

Think of the passwords that you use at the moment. Are they based around dates, clever combinations of letters and numbers or are they strong empowering words with resonance? A positive mindset will bring the rewards you need so let it be apparent in every area. The next time you are asked to set a password, choose a word that will inspire and put you in the successful frame of mind. How about choosing a word that reflects a winning situation, such as the name of your university, your mentor, your first customer, your innovation, your idea? How about a word that describes you in the future, millionaire, gold medalist, professor, chief executive, powerful. Get the idea? Use this as a chance to allow success to seep into every corner of your life, even into the hard disc of your computer.

Meetings

Meetings with colleagues, customers and other groups are your opportunity to shine. This doesn't mean it is your chance to dominate the conversation and it doesn't mean to say you sit thinking furiously in the corner, loving every moment but not contributing. This is the forum where people will decide what they think about you and as you only get one chance to create a first impression and then lots of others to confirm it, what can you do to make sure that you get it right?

Think of an occasion when you got on well with someone, when you were in deep rapport, working well, finding it easy to talk and to get on. Picture yourself in that situation. What was happening? Did you sit near each other, did you speak at the same pace, at the same volume? Did you sit back quietly with a distance between you or did you move closer into each other's body space? Good rapport is not just about what you are saying. It is also about how you say it and what you look like when it is being said. Just think how useful this will be to you in the work situation. You will improve how you deal with your boss, your colleagues, your customers, your suppliers, your students.

Non Face to face Communication

Somehow it always seems easier to communicate if you are face to face, seeing someone eye to eye, working hand in glove. Even our everyday language encourages us to get in front of people. The fast pace of modern communications, however, ensures that it is possible to get on with things and to make decisions without needing to meet. Suddenly you need to make strong connections with people and you are missing the physiology that makes up so much of rapport. Instead of focusing on what you don't have, let's see what you do have.

It seems that we all e-mail, both in personal as well as business life. Letters are becoming intriguing relics of a bygone age whereas e-mails are flying into the inbox 24 hours a day, seven days a week. This e-mail correspondence can be measured and considered, a carefully crafted piece of prose that has been thoughtfully created in order to send the right message to the right person. Every word will have been selected and placed in the right place in order to create the appropriate impact. This e-mail will be a model of excellence in what is an imperfect electronic world. Most e-mails will be hastily put together in lots of different ways. They may have been fired out late at night when you are tired or in a rush, hastily sent out via a Blackberry when standing in a queue or on a street corner or rushed out in the half hour you have allocated for clearing your inbox first thing in the morning. They may even have been sent out when you are angry, fed up, upset or on your way to bed after a meal that included a bottle of wine.

As a result, the e-mail that you think you have sent may not be the e-mail that is received. Nuances that you had not intended may not be there, frustrations and emotions that you had not intended to disclose may well be apparent and the result of this e-mail communication is not what you had hoped for. E-mails that are sent late at night are likely to lack the fine tuning of one that is carefully crafted. George, someone I was coaching, received an e-mail sent by his boss at midnight on Saturday. It was short and to the point: 'We need to schedule an urgent meeting for Monday at 10 am. Clear your diary and make sure you are there'. George's weekend was ruined. He was convinced that he was going to be fired or made redundant or hauled over the coals. He went into the office to discover that his boss had been reflecting on a major project that needed to be launched and had decided that George would lead it. Re-reading the e-mail, he admitted that he had only conveyed the urgency of the meeting and had opened the door to uncertainty and doubt.

Unlike telephone conversations or personal meetings, records of e-mails are there forever. They can and will be forwarded to other people and will be used to demonstrate either your efficiency or your inadequacies. Knowing this, are you sure that you want to e-mail? Is this the easiest way or the best way to say what you want? Ask yourself if you are slipping into e-mail habits whether you can do it better face to face or by a telephone call. It can take ten minutes to have an e-mail exchange that could be handled by a quick two minute telephone conversation. This is an opportunity to engage with a colleague or a customer and it is also a way to save time in the working day and get more done. Great people do more and e-mailing is an opportunity to use all of your skills to show how valuable you are.

In e-mailing, you could make sure that the subject line reflects the message you want to send. Make a habit of creating a new e mail rather than pressing 'Reply'. This means you will then have the chance to create a compelling subject line such as:

♦ 'Friendly reminder from your favourite supplier'
♦ 'Six ideas for your next project'
♦ 'Grateful thanks for all your help'
♦ 'Appreciation of your work to date'

These then constitute a positive anchor, reminding the receiver of you every time that they look at their inbox. Equally powerfully you can use them to nudge and remind about less pleasant matters 'Outstanding invoices – overdue by a week', 'Awaiting payment on Tuesday', 'Your late delivery'.

Signing off

Now look at the way your e-mail ends. Do you have a standard sign off or have you created something that stands out, makes you noticed and makes you memorable?

Someone I have worked with through the years is a gifted Coach and team builder who always signed off her e-mails with a quotation from Henry Thoreau. Underneath her contact details she wrote 'Go confidently in the direction of your dreams.' One day a friend sent her a card she had found and she was suddenly faced with the whole of the quotation. It was 'Go confidently in the direction of your dreams. Live the life you have imagined.' It was an enlightening moment. The next week she had arranged a trip to France to look at properties that she might consider buying. When she came back she announced that she had achieved her life's dream, she had bought a chateau in Provence, complete with essential turret. She sold her house in London and moved to her chateau. She followed the dream and created a new reality.

Look at your sign off and think what you can do to change it. Make a mental note to review it and change it regularly. Others will notice it and look forward to what you are going to do next.

Timing and structure

There are ways to time your e-mail message that will show you are in rapport. The e-mail that arrives half an hour before an essential meeting will be valued much more than one that comes half an hour after it has finished. You can show that you are thinking of the other person and make sure that you are expressing it appropriately.

When you construct the message think about the attachments and present them in a way that makes it easy for the recipient to file away. If you attach a file entitled 'Proposal', this will just create work for someone. Call it 'Proposal from XYZ to ABC dated 021010' and you will be showing consideration, one of the important elements of rapport.

The phone call and the e-mail

There is a moment when these two are at odds with each other. Have you ever been on the telephone to someone when you have been sitting in front of your computer and suddenly an exciting e-mail pops into your inbox? How irresistible is that wonderful enticing e-mail with its seductive Subject matter. ... What do you do? You open it and skim read it because the person you are talking to, probably me, is droning on at length about something tedious. After all, they can't see you and they won't know what you are doing, will they?

Wrong. People who are on the phone always know when the person they are speaking to has been distracted and is not listening. The result will be that rapport vanishes and irritation will take its place. Although you may have other priorities in your life, I don't like being reminded of them so I will be offended and you will have to build bridges.

To prevent yourself from being tempted and distracted, close off your e mail, do not browse the internet while someone is talking and ensure that you are sending total attention down the telephone line. It will reap rewards.

Answerphones

Have you ever paid attention to the messages that people leave on their answerphones? If you listen hard you can tell what frame of mind they were in when they recorded it, where they were located, how much they had rehearsed it and how much thought had gone into it.

Be determined to focus on much more than the language content, write out what you want to say, carefully choosing the right modalities, stand up or sit up straight and practice the tone and the volume you plan to use. Make sure that this recorded message sends the image that you want to project.

Remember: We are always communicating and the meaning of communication is the response you receive. Change what and how you say things and suddenly the response you receive will be more than you hope for.

Decision Making

HOW TO MAKE THE BEST DECISIONS TO FUEL YOUR SUCCESS

"We are all in charge of our minds and therefore our results. The law of cause and effect"

The most important step in managing your career and your progression is to make the decision that you are in control of your own life and how you react to what happens to you. If you are not running your own life, then it means someone else is and this places you in the position of being the victim. People who are in charge of their own destiny decide what happens to them and they do not allow themselves to be at the mercy of events. Real control is choosing how to respond to situations that genuinely are outside your control. Although you can't change the event itself, you can control how to respond to them. These people, in NLP terms, are defined as being at 'Cause'. The ones who feel helpless in the wake of unwelcome events turn themselves into victims and are known as being at 'Effect'.

Cause and Effect

That the actions of others can have consequences for you is an extension of the theory that a butterfly flapping its wings in one part of the world can cause a tornado somewhere else. In business terms you need to be the person who is flapping your wings as the alternative is to be embroiled in a tornado. It is a harsh fact of business life that the unexpected will happen and you will need to adjust and adapt. Everyone has a boss and therefore you can be the unwilling or the willing recipient of the consequences of change. The ultimate example of being on the receiving end of the worst kind of decision is being made redundant. Here, however, you still have a choice, either to accept the decision and choose to create a new and better life or to rail against fate, complain and become a victim.

If you are at Effect you relinquish power to others. Choice is no longer yours. You are bending to the will of others as you have chosen to adopt the philosophy that it is not your fault. Someone else is driving your bus so you will end up where they take you. Life is out of your control and you are at the mercy of others.

The person who remains at Cause is the one who chooses to believe that whatever life throws at them, they will be in control of their own destiny. Whilst it is not possible to stop events in life, it is possible to change your response.

I was working with a company that was reducing its cost base by making posts redundant. Two people in the senior management team found themselves out of a job. The decision was made purely on the basis of cost reduction and had nothing to do with their performance. Bob, the Operations Director, understood the reasons and although he was shocked and upset, he stayed calm and professional throughout. As a result he negotiated excellent severance terms, retained the goodwill of all around and he found people wanted to introduce him to contacts who could be helpful. In forthcoming job interviews this positive attitude shone through and he made a good impression. It was not long before he found another job.

However, Matthew, the Sales Director who was made redundant, reacted very differently. He was bitter, angry, upset and he lashed out at everyone. He was difficult, emotional and made every encounter difficult for his employer. As a result people dreaded their meetings with him and they were constantly braced for trouble with him. This inevitably was what they found and the Sales Director was given what he was entitled to and no more. A bitter taste was left in everyone's mouth and they were thankful when he left the business. Matthew found people were reluctant to return his calls and his resentment and bitterness came through at interviews. Bob, by being at cause, chose to accept the decision and find a direction for his life. Matthew was at effect and lost his sense of purpose.

Statements of People at Effect

♦ My boss dislikes me
♦ No one ever lets me speak
♦ I can't help it
♦ It's not my fault
♦ If it hadn't been for the poor team effort, I would have succeeded
♦ Manufacturing always let me down
♦ The people working for me never deliver
♦ The sales team gave me terrible forecasts
♦ Everyone else has been to university but I haven't
♦ They made me feel inadequate
♦ The train was late so I missed the meeting
♦ My alarm clock didn't go off so I slept in
♦ They never included me

And the list goes on. In truth they are all excuses about why something has not happened. Although it may well be true that the train was late or the sales team always give shocking forecasts, the truly decisive person who runs their own life and is not at the mercy of chance events is someone who anticipates potential problems or they resolve them rather than collecting them as excuses.

Statements of people at Cause

♦ I will get that done
♦ I will get in touch with him
♦ I have designed an agenda
♦ I will work with the team to resolve the issue about the forecast

♦ I made a mistake and I will find a way to fix it
♦ I will work with my boss to get his buy in
♦ I sent the wrong item and I will now make sure I send the right one
♦ I filled the car with petrol instead of diesel because I was not paying attention
♦ I missed the meeting because I set off too late

I am sure you can see the difference. People who are at cause recognize that blaming others is unproductive. Solutions come from people who acknowledge where they have gone wrong personally and how they can take charge of their own destiny. This is the path to improvement.

Decision making and procrastination

If you have a job that you love in every single part, then you are very lucky. A universal experience is that jobs vary in their appeal. There are parts you love doing, some things you are OK with and things you are less keen on. All of them need to be done, regardless of your attitude to them. It is also inevitable that what you have not done, half done or totally ignored will be much more visible to your boss and your peers than your successes. Some people hate routine administration, the VAT return, making difficult telephone calls, keeping pace with routine e-mails, filling in time sheets. What is easy for you can be tough for someone else. Likes and dislikes are personal and irrational. The impact of paying attention to negative feelings and leaving tasks undone can be catastrophic for careers.

One of my clients has a brilliant manager of a sales team called Dan. He achieved results that were outstanding. He was liked by all and every month his bonuses got bigger. His boss noticed that he was getting into work earlier and earlier and thought that this was because he was becoming even more motivated to get work done.

Eventually the Finance department flagged up to the boss that the debtor days were getting greater and that cash flow was tight. People were not paying their bills. An investigation that culminated in searching Dan's desk produced piles of correspondence from dissatisfied clients who were refusing to pay their bills because of the poor quality of work that Dan's team was producing. Dan couldn't face up to difficult customer issues and his response was to bury his head in the sand. It all caught up with him and he was dismissed.

Unless you are completely in control of every element of your working day, procrastination will creep in, leaving you vulnerable to the accusation that 'You just don't get things off the page and you never get things done.'

Avoidance of procrastination

First of all, take the time to be totally honest about what you do and what you choose not to do, i.e. avoid. Write a list of key tasks that make up your working week. Then consider each task and ask yourself 'How effective am I in doing this task?' Then ask yourself 'Have there been occasions when I have avoided doing this task?' and finally ask yourself 'What is important about this task for the functioning of the business?'

Give each task and each question a score on a scale of 1 to 10:

Description of the task	Do you like doing it?	Do you avoid it?	Is it a priority for business?

Now look at the list and check for a mismatch. If there is a disparity between what you are doing and what the business needs, then there is a fair chance on a number of occasions you let someone down or you fail to maximize an opportunity that is in front of you.

If you are not seen to be making decisions, you will be thought to be indecisive, dithering, wavering, uncertain, unsure, or lacking in confidence, all perceived to be flaws in someone who aspires to be a leader. Some leaders appear to be fearless and sometimes it is better to ask for forgiveness than to ask for permission. It is safe to assume that most decisions you make will be good ones. The decisions that prove to be ones that result in problems, whether it is taking in the wrong kind of order, moving to the wrong job or employing the wrong person tend to be the best possible learning experiences. Do not be afraid of getting things wrong as this is the way to ensure better decision making in the future. Make a decision today because you can always make another one tomorrow.

Leadership

Gareth James of People Plus says:

'Successful leadership is more to do with what you inspire others to do than what you do yourself. The real attributes of leaders are their ability to surround themselves with the right people and retain them, to build effective teams, to listen and to be capable of making decisions on their own – but normally after consultation, not without it.'

Making better decisions

People have very different ways of making decisions and generally the best decisions are those that are made incorporating every perspective and as many points of view as possible. If you are working on your own, deciding what you need to do and without any access to the ideas of others, here are some simple techniques to help you broaden your own horizons. You may naturally be someone who looks at the bigger picture. Your style may be to see possibilities, patterns opportunities and yet miss the detail that could be the key to success or failure. In NLP terms, you would be described as someone who chunks up – you take information in big chunks. On the other hand, you might be someone who likes to get straight into the details, looking at precise and specific points, liking to amass as much information as possible. The danger here is that you might miss the big picture and opportunities might slip past. This in NLP terms is known as chunking down.

Whatever your natural preference is, you can choose to incorporate both elements into your everyday decisions, bringing up to a conscious level that you need to chunk up and you need to chunk down. Of course, if you are sitting in a strategy meeting where people are exploring ideas and possibilities, no one will thank you for getting down into what is at that point irrelevant detail. Context is everything so check that what you are doing fits the purpose.

When you buy a flat pack piece of furniture from somewhere like IKEA, how do you go about building it? Do you tip all the pieces onto the floor and start working out how they go together? Or are you someone who gets out the instructions, reads them carefully and works their way through them step by step? Both ways bring results but the combined approach could save time and effort.

Chunking up or chunking down?

Sometimes it is important to see a bigger picture and look at it from a more strategic perspective and sometimes it is better to get into the detail. The best decision makers are those who are skilled in both areas and who have the acumen to know when it is appropriate to use a different approach.

Chunking up to the big picture

Think how useful this will be when you are faced with something you are doubtful about, when you can't see the point in doing something or when you are simply trying to stretch your boundaries. Ask yourself the following questions:

♦ What is this an example of?
♦ For what purpose would we do this? (and then keep asking it until you get to the heart of the issue)
♦ What is your intention?

Chunking down to the detail

When you know that your ideas are going to be challenged for the operational practicality or their commercial viability, make sure that before you float your ideas you have robustly tested them. Do this by asking questions that drill down to detail such as:

♦ What precisely?
♦ How specifically?
♦ How exactly?
♦ What are examples of this?
♦ Can I put it on a spreadsheet?
♦ What are the costings?
♦ What are the timings?

Become a nitpicker because if you don't, someone else will and if you are not able to answer the detailed questions, you will be creating doubt and uncertainty. Not everyone is a natural detail person but by making it part of how you manage, your decisions will be more rounded and better formed.

When you look at your team members, notice who paints with a broader brush and who lets the details escape them. Make sure that your feedback to them includes the requirements for specifics and detail.

Believing in others

The single most important decision any of us will ever have to make is whether or not to believe the Universe is friendly.

The best decisions are made by people who have the highest expectations of others. Cynical people who expect to be let down by those around them are usually not disappointed. The belief that people will do a good job and want to do their best will reinforce your decisions and give you the confidence to move forward and be brave.

Say what you mean and get what you want

Successful people think before they speak and ensure that they frame their language carefully so that they get what they want. Their choice of words produces the desired results and does not leave them wondering what went wrong in the process. To be seen as a leader in the organization, you need to be seen as someone who can make decisions and then convey the reason for that decision to others. This will be achieved by assuming responsibility for the communication and being certain that there will be no drift of purpose along the way.

Clarity

The first step to clarity of purpose is to say it the way that you want it. When you say exactly what you want, stating it specifically and stating it in the positive, you remove all ambiguity. You will be making your own position very clear on whatever the topic might be and there will no room at all for misunderstanding.

Remove any ambiguity so rather than saying, 'I don't like some of the foods on this menu', you will formulate it as 'I prefer some of the fish based dishes rather than red meat.'

You could say 'I expect this work to be delivered by the end of September' rather than saying that 'I don't mind when I get it so long as it gives me time to review it.'

Necessity and possibility

There are phrases and words that open the door to doubt and uncertainty. These are words that imply some kind of necessity – words like:

♦ should
♦ must
♦ ought to
♦ have to
♦ needs to
♦ it is necessary

They carry with them an implication of necessity and they beg the question 'Why do I and who says so?' When someone uses them to you, the correct way to challenge is to ask

'What would happen if you did?' or 'What would happen if you didn't?'

Then there are the words that imply possibility or impossibility that are:

♦ can /can't
♦ will/won't
♦ may/may not

The words of impossibility can be show stoppers in a meeting unless they are quickly defused by questions such as 'What prevents you?' or 'What would happen if you did?'

When you are putting across your point, use positives and avoid 'but'. When you are answering someone, if you say 'I can see your point of view but ...' you are instantly in a situation of challenge and disagreement. By changing this to 'I can see your point of view and' you will be making exactly the same point without breaking the rapport that you have already established. It is easier to work in an environment where you are smoothly taking people with you rather than creating an atmosphere of tension and conflict.

An agreement framework

To win the day you want to get people's agreement so that they endorse your decision. Hypnotic language patterns are subtle and speak to the unconscious mind, inviting the understanding and the agreement of others. The most effective in this situation are the phrases that would seem to be 'mind reading.'

Think about the impact of some of the following:

♦ You are probably aware
♦ I can tell you share my thoughts (feelings) on this
♦ I know you believe
♦ I am sure you have similar experiences
♦ I realize that you already know what I am telling you
♦ I see that you know what the problem is
♦ I have heard that this is something you are interested in

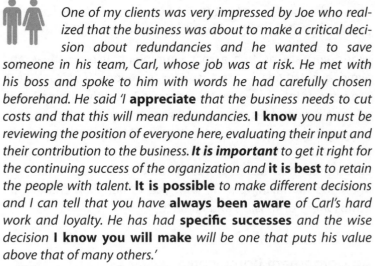

One of my clients was very impressed by Joe who realized that the business was about to make a critical decision about redundancies and he wanted to save someone in his team, Carl, whose job was at risk. He met with his boss and spoke to him with words he had carefully chosen beforehand. He said 'I **appreciate** *that the business needs to cut costs and that this will mean redundancies.* **I know** *you must be reviewing the position of everyone here, evaluating their input and their contribution to the business.* **It is important** *to get it right for the continuing success of the organization and* **it is best** *to retain the people with talent.* **It is possible** *to make different decisions and I can tell that you have* **always been aware** *of Carl's hard work and loyalty. He has had* **specific successes** *and the wise decision* **I know you will make** *will be one that puts his value above that of many others.'*

This was not confrontational but was positioned to establish rapport, assume a positive intent and get the results he wanted. After further discussion, Joe won and Carl's job was saved.

Another linguistic technique is one where you will end your sentence with a question that can only be answered in the way you want it. The simplest way is to end with 'and isn't this easy for you?' 'and you are bound to be able to achieve it in the timescales, aren't you? Overcome potential barriers and objections by assuming the agreement 'You can, can you not?'

Getting the answer you want: The Double Bind

The best way to ensure that a decision goes your way is to stack it up beforehand in your favour. It is far easier to influence the outcome by thinking things through in advance than it is to step in as a firefighter when decisions have already been made. One way to do this is via the double bind which, when used skilfully, gives the wonderful illusion of choice. The old joke is that of the salesman who presents the order form for you to sign and says 'Your pen or mine?' The option of not signing is not there. This technique is something you would use when you are facing someone who has trouble in making decisions or, worse still, makes the decision that you don't want. In order to progress through the organization, you need to be seen to be making good decisions and these also need to be bought into by others to make them happen. If you create a plan that people ignore, then you are not likely to go far. By creating an illusion of choice but in fact there is no choice, you achieve your objectives.

The way that this works in practice is for example, if you know that your Project Manager, your boss, a colleague is avoiding the one to one that you need to happen, you need to be able to pin them down. Rather than saying 'When would you like to meet me this week?' which invites the response 'I am too busy this week', change the question to something that provides the choice of two viable alternatives, one of which will not be 'I am too busy'. For example, you could say, 'Would you able to meet me on Thursday late afternoon or would you prefer Friday morning?.' Certainly do not fall into the trap of saying 'Can you make a meeting on Thursday or are you too busy?.' Look – you have given them an escape route! This careful double bind structure puts a stop to open ended options and leads to a fixed date.

A car sales person might say 'Do you prefer this car or would you prefer it in a different colour?' The third option, not buying the car at all, is not there as a choice. A variation on this theme is 'Would you prefer to pay cash or banker's draft?'

Another way of phrasing it is 'Do you prefer Model A or do you prefer Model B?' rather than 'which one do you prefer?' which allows for a third option, 'Neither'. This careful use of questions where you are providing the right answer with the question is one that will accelerate decision making and avoid procrastination

Practise and be perfect
These techniques will need to be practised and need to be integrated seamlessly into your conversation. If they appear awkward or stilted, people will be on the alert as the rapport will have been broken. The conscious mind will intervene and your pathway to unconscious acquiescence will be blocked.

> Remember: Accepting that you are 100% in charge of life and so you are 100% in charge of your success. Deciding that will mean you put yourself forward to achieve it, constantly striving to play above your game.

Flexibility

HOW TO DEVELOP THE FLEXIBILITY YOU NEED TO SUCCEED

> "The person with the greatest flexibility controls the system and will have the greatest influence. There are no resistant people. There are just inflexible communicators."

If you are a flexible person, it means you will have the skill to adopt more views than your own. If you stick rigidly to your own view, your own thoughts and your own way of doing things, then that means other people around you, who may not agree with you, are obliged either to accept that you are right, and therefore change their opinions, or there will be a discussion, a disagreement and possibly an argument. There are many perspectives to all situations and the team member who is willing and able to embrace more than their own point of view is the one who will be in the strongest position and will be held in highest regard. If you limit your views and attitudes then you are handing the competitive edge to someone else. Business leaders are people who have the most variety in their behaviour and who do not have a standard response.

Going from good to great means having to take this leap in terms of mindset and thinking style. How often have you been in a meeting with someone who is clearly not listening to you but is merely mentally rehearsing what they are going to say as soon as they get a chance? Talking is your chance to express what you think. Listening is your opportunity to hear views that may be radically different from your own. Remembering that the best decisions are those that incorporate the experience, intelligence, opinions and vision of others, how do you ensure that you are sufficiently flexible to facilitate excellent decision making?

Remember an occasion when you have found yourself at loggerheads with someone, both of you convinced that you are right and refusing to give way. It could be about a marketing strategy, it could be deciding the best way to spend the budget. It could as simple as deciding where to hold the office party. Merely reiterating your own opinion will not move the situation to a mutually satisfactory conclusion. I am not suggesting capitulation as a way forward. I am not advocating the kind of compromise that satisfies no one. What I want you to consider is that there is not always just one right answer. There could be a number of good answers and variations on those themes. In order to reach that range of possibilities, you need to make the decision right now that you are prepared to seek them out actively and to be willing to accept that they could be valid.

Gareth James, Director of People Plus, says

'Decisions are made on the basis of perceptions, so manage perceptions. Perception is projection. People perceptions are based on what you say and do – if you want to change the perception, change the projection.'

How will this be helpful to you? It will help you to understand the mindset of your boss, colleagues, customers, suppliers. If you work in customer service, it will help you understand why someone is upset and annoyed. These different insights will then help you develop a plan to put things right in a way that otherwise you might not have imagined. Although your boss is likely to value you for your determination, it is likely that he will be very frustrated with what he perceives to be stubbornness.

If you are being asked to do something that you find unpalatable or difficult, it will help you to have a much clearer understanding of why someone is asking you to do it. For example, if you are being asked to make cost savings and make people in your department redundant or if you are part of a team where others are losing their jobs, gain a true grasp of the reasons why this is happening and you will find it easier to adjust to a changing workplace.

Matthew Alsop, Managing Director of FCSPD Support, says:

'Be as flexible as you can be within your personal circumstance. For example, if there is overtime on offer don't let yourself be the last person to volunteer or stand out because you never say yes and offer to help. The money will always come in handy. Flexibility is a very valuable asset in a company's employees when times get difficult.'

Training yourself to move across perspectives and positions (or Perceptual Positions as NLP likes to call it) will give you the greater mental scope you need to grow inside your organization.

Perceptual positions – how it works

1. Self

This is the easiest one. This is your perspective, it is who you are. It is seeing the world through your eyes, hearing what is being said through your ears and feeling what is happening through your own way of taking information on board. This is where life is comfortable.

Imagine you are sitting in a chair looking at a situation that you have wrapped up and put in a box in front of you. You can now see it through your own eyes and you can focus on what it looks like. Consider for a minute what you can't see. You can't view it from behind or above. You can't see it from underneath.

You can only see what your limited perspective allows. Whatever you are thinking of doing, recognize now that it will not be the best decision ever. Would you buy a house based on a photo of the outside? You are likely to want floor plans, a picture of the garden, an overhead picture and a map that shows what it is surrounded by. What is it that you don't know and what you can't see?

2. Other

This is the opportunity to experience the situation in a new way, developing the ability to see and to hear and to feel things differently. How many times have you wished you could hear what was being said behind closed doors? This is a way for you to open the door and experience it for yourself.

Put another chair in the room and stand up and go and move onto it. This is your chance to shift into someone else's shoes. You are now in a physically different space so you have a new vista, a different horizon and you see other people in a different light. Not only that, you can see yourself and be a very interested observer of what is going on. This time you are participating from a different angle.

3. Impartial Observer

We have all wished on occasions that we could be the fly on the wall, the person who can see what is happening but without being seen and without needing to make a contribution. Place a third chair in the room and this is the place where the independent person sits, the one who notices what is happening in relationships and conversations but is emotionally detached, not part of the decision-making process. This observer is interested in the outcome and can see impartially what is going on. This is like the umpire in the tennis match who wants to see that the game is played fairly according to the rules and without any vested interest in one or the other winning. Ideally, the Chairman on a board of directors is this Impartial Observer, the person who takes the heat out of debate and brings people back to objective facts.

How does it work for you?

Now you have the technique, how do you apply it to a real situation? Accepting that there is no failure here, only valuable feedback and insights that will help you grow, think of a current work-based situation that is causing you concern. It could be a customer complaining about quality, it could be resentment at the Finance Department's latest edict on cost cutting, it could be a refusal to give you a salary increase or to move your status from temporary to permanent.

Now you have that specific situation clear in your head, set out three chairs in your imaginary room. If you have the time and space, why not do it in reality at your kitchen table or in an empty meeting room at work?

Set up the chairs in a triangular format about two metres apart. Label each chair as 'Self', 'Other' and 'Impartial Observer'.

Step 1

Either sit in the chair or stand alongside it if you prefer and look at the chair of the 'other'. You will know who this 'other' is as you are seeking a solution to a specific problem. Thinking of the work-based situation that you have described and knowing that you are seeking to change yourself and not the other, ask yourself the question 'How does this behaviour affect me?' You will be clear about what you want and what you think so this is your opportunity to look at the person, ask the question and work out what the impact is.

Step 2

Stand up, apply the mental windscreen wiper to clear your mind and now go over to the 'other' chair, remembering that this is someone you have identified specifically, a customer, a colleague or someone who is part of this difficult situation. Sit on the chair or stand behind it and step into their shoes while you are doing it. You are now going to see the world as they see it, that is to say you are associated and you will hear and you will feel what they feel. Look at the chair marked 'self' and ask the question 'How is that behaviour affecting me?' Remember to see yourself through the eyes of the other and willingly listen to the insights you will be seeing and feeling.

Step 3

Clearing your mind again through the application of that windscreen wiper that breaks state, move to the third chair, that of the Impartial Observer. You can now see both of the discussions and you are dissociated for what you are going to observe, what you can hear and what you feel. Pay careful note to what is going on with both and ask the question 'How is this behaviour affecting the decision?' As you have been on both the first and second chair, you will be able to integrate both viewpoints and develop a third perspective that carries with it the advantages of both.

Now move the chairs in so that they are only one metre apart. Repeat the entire exercise above. This time things will be more immediate and more striking, bringing with them more learning and better insights. It will provide answers to things that have been puzzling you and help you create a new framework for a decision.

Result

By giving yourself different perspectives through mental discipline, you make better decisions and increase your value to the organization. It will allow you to be the person who is ready to take responsibility for the personal conflicts and disagreements that occur all the time in organizations.

Preparing for the unexpected

Have you ever found yourself in a meeting when suddenly the spotlight turns onto you and you are asked a question that you can't answer? You may have reams of data in front of you and in your head and yet you are paralyzed when a question is put to you. It might be something simple or something complex. Whatever it is, the answer just won't come. You are on the spot, the room is silent and people are waiting. How do you react?

With no preparation for such a scenario, the danger is that you could freeze, your mind goes blank, you get flustered and you give the appearance that you are not on top of your job and you are not in control. It has happened to all of us. Skilful use of resources will mean that you can manage the situation and retain your reputation for being knowledgeable and in control.

1. Practice regaining a calm state of mind. Think of a time when you were certain of your facts. Remember a time when you were excelling, when you knew the answer and no one else did. Think where you were, who else was there. Regain the intensity of that feeling, that rush of satisfaction that you knew the answer. Hear the voice in your head, that positive, reassuring voice that tells you that you are right. At the moment when you are in the peak state of regaining the strength of all those feelings, create a physical anchor. Do this by either pinching your left ear, tapping your foot, pressing the nail on the little finger of your right hand. Do something that you will be comfortable with and use it as an instant capability to recall that calm, knowledgeable and confident state. Although there is no magic solution to giving answers to tough questions, sometimes the mind fills with panic and the voice in your head is clamouring that it does not know the answer. This is the way to regain control, allowing the space for the right answer to float up from your unconscious mind.

2. If you actually do not know the answer, then use skilful language to deflect the situation. Great people are not in a panic, out of control or looking blank in meetings. Using the calm state that you know how to access, decide how you

will respond. You could say 'Good point and one I haven't got all the details for right now. I will e-mail to all straight after the meeting and I will also include (think of something pertinent).' Distract and move on.

The fast and flexible thinker will be able to change the focus of the debate and will do so in a constructive way.

Clare Howard of Academy 28 says:

'Never admit to being a Luddite, a technophobe or a snob whether it be intellectual, cultural, musical, tastes and brands.'

A flexible working environment

Is the best way to being sure you are in the right place for the right task. If you plan to settle down to an uninterrupted period of hard work, getting through paper mountains and long lists of telephone calls, then a noisy and vibrant office will be too distracting and you will be stacking yourself up for failure. A quiet office or a day operating from home will be the best option. Equally, if you are looking for the input of others and are keen to hear what else is going on in the world, tuning in to what others know, then it is easy to see that these facts are best collected round 'the water cooler.' Informal chats and exchanges in the office can give you interesting data that will give you important clues about what you could be doing. Be careful to avoid the lure of 'working from home', as although it might be tempting to save time by missing a commute to work, you run the risk of becoming an invisible worker and an invisible worker is difficult to value. You will end up working in a vacuum and no one will know if you are good or great.

The best way to be noticed as a flexible and interested person in the business is to get engaged with different aspects and divisions. Just because you work in, say, finance or quality, it does not exclude you from learning about other aspects of the business and adding value in different ways.

A flexible approach

Some of us like to work in a systematic and logical way, knowing what needs to be done and working in a straight line towards it. This brings the advantage that you will be seen to be conscientious, organized, always on time, on top of your game and with nothing left to chance. You will have lists of things to do and you will work through them in a thorough way. Meetings will be booked way ahead, plans in place, agendas distributed and resources allocated. You know what you need to do and you make sure you get there. For you, there is a sense of relief in knowing that a decision has been made, a path defined and life is clear cut. Those of you who are familiar with the Myers Briggs Type Indicator will recognize this kind of 'J' description. For those of you who are not familiar with the MBTI®, you will be fascinated by how it works. The MBTI® is a personality questionnaire based on Jungian Type that has been developed over many years. It looks at how a person perceives the world and how they prefer to interact with others. It also helps individuals and teams improve their working and personal relationships in a positive and constructive way.

On the other hand, you might be someone who loves choice and different options. You know what you have to do and you like exploring, opening up possibilities and potential. You thrive on the adrenalin of creating numerous paths and you are rewarded by the journey rather than by arrival. This 'P' person in Myers Briggs terms loves variety, choice and feels a certain regret when decisions are made as this closes off so many other opportunities.

Wherever you sit on the J /P spectrum, you will be able to see the advantages that come with both preferences. Flexible people see more than others and adapt to changing circumstances.

Remember: though that however flexible you might like to be, there comes a point of commitment. Decisions need to be made, choices exercised and what you have decided communicated to your team.

Team Player

HOW TO WORK THROUGH LOGICAL LEVELS OF CHANGE TO GET TO WHERE YOU NEED TO BE

"Behind every behaviour there is a positive intent"

A key principle of NLP is the belief that we are all doing the best we can. No one comes to work to be difficult, to cause conflict or to do a bad job. Everyone loves a team player. However good you may be in your job, you need to be someone who is a cohesive part of the whole. Some do it quite naturally whereas for others the independent route is the most natural and instinctive.

It will be very strange if you manage to get through an entire career without ever having to attend some form of team building programme. Some of them will be better than others and all of them will bring benefits of one sort or another if approached with the right mindset. The indication, therefore, is that to be a team player is a good thing and if you don't do it easily, you can now focus on how to improve.

The best teams are those that work well together, each bringing their strength to the team and ensuring that the combination of the parts is significantly more than the whole. The challenge with this can be that sometimes it is difficult to work with people who are different. Difference is what makes the team succeed and being unable to accept the personal challenge that this difference brings can cause people not to work well together. By focusing on what you can do for the business rather than what it can do for you, you make yourself indispensable. Great people are needed by the business so make sure that your contribution is valuable and that they cannot do without you. This creates more positive and powerful dynamics than you being in a position where you need the job more than the business needs what you do.

Change through Logical Levels

In order to be aligned with the team, it is important that you should in the first place feel that this business and its values are the right place for you to be. If you feel uncomfortable, ill at ease or unhappy with the company's values, you need to work out why. A much better starting point would be to have identified what is important to you for you and be sure that you are in the right place where you will succeed. Robert Dilts, a leader in the field of NLP, developed a structural model to allow for growth and change and this is what Heather Summers and I used as a platform to develop our Stairway of Happiness in our book *The Book of Happiness – Brilliant ideas to transform your life*. By visiting www.switchtosuccess.co.uk you will be able to do the Happiness questionnaire and see the logical stages towards achieving it.

Using the same model and accepting that the ultimate goal is what you have already established as you began to read the book, something that will include improved performance in your job and the recognition that goes with it, there are clear steps towards to it.

By working through these steps now, you will have the opportunity to identify the key areas in your life where you may feel slightly ill at ease or jarring out of alignment. This will allow you to see where the change needs to take place, removing barriers and highlighting the blind spots that perhaps have held you back in the past. Not only that, you will be able to use this model and process of thinking to help people in your team and in your business. By aligning everyone so that you are all synchronized, working with the same values to a clear goal, the business's results will improve and you will be more valued than before. Good to great can only be achieved by bringing the team with you, unless you have a very unusual role where you exist in total isolation and your results are stand alone with no influence or impact from others. By working closely with your team you will be able to explore what individuals want and use this knowledge to improve all round performance. When the team has realigned itself, there will be a greater confidence about its capabilities and this will be able to shine through.

When you look at this model and you are using it for change, it is important to be sure to be working at the level above where you are in order to have the resources in place. For example, if you are working on your Surroundings, you need also to be developing the right Behaviour in order to get there. In other words, you may need to take action and change some of the things you do (Behaviour) or increase your Skills and Capabilities, change your Beliefs or reassess your Identity.

Logical level of change – Step One – Surroundings

Your surroundings are what you see, hear, feel and think when you look around you. This is the physical place where you live and where you work. It is your daily commute, the office where you work, the place where you park your car and the physical context in which you are operating.

James had a high-flying job in the City and lived with his wife and children in Battersea. He loved his job and was very highly paid. One of his children had some learning difficulties and they found the perfect school for him in Yorkshire. He and his wife decided that the family would move North and that James would commute weekly. He bought a tiny flat in Clerkenwell and the solution seemed to have been found.

After a year of this James was at the end of his tether. He was exhausted from the commute and he hated being on his own during the week. As a result, his working hours extended and he was miserable. He decided to resign, sell the flat in London and job seek in the North. After twelve months of fruitless job hunting, he decided to accept a job with a much lower salary and to cut living costs. He changed his environment by adapting his behaviour.

I carried out research with a group of graduates who all have two years plus work experience. They are in diverse sectors that include banking, the medical profession, teaching and advertising. I asked them what had the greatest impact on their performance at work and what was the one thing they would change if they could. Every single one commented on the environment, on the length of the commute, the inflexible working hours and the offices and area where they were.

If you are only experiencing a mild dissatisfaction with your working environment, you can take steps by yourself to change it. You can move your desk, redecorate the room, brighten it up, bring in a radio or turn one off if it is annoying you. However, if this is fundamentally wrong, you will need to consider radical change to be able to achieve all of your potential.

Ask yourself the question 'Am I where I want to be?' If you are in the right place, working for the right company in the right location, surrounded by people with whom you have shared values, then you will be on the high road to success. If you are at odds with any of these, you are building on sand.

If you are the owner of the business or the Managing Director, take the time to look at the working environment you are giving your employees. Is it a place where people want to work? What improvements could you make that would be appreciated? Some people gain goodwill from their people by providing free fruit, Pilates classes, gym membership, a subsidized lunch or frequent staff outings. People need more than just a suitable physical environment; it needs to be an empowering one where people can feel a sense of purpose and achievement in their work.

Logical level of change – Step two – Behaviour

The way you behave includes what you do, how you do it, who you do it with and how others behave with you. It is also about what you think, what you say and how you say it. Behaviour is under your control so it is about taking responsibility for your own actions and for the way in which you respond to the everyday situations in life that come your way. You are 100% responsible for your behaviour. Remember that the next step of logical level is Capabilities so you need to consider your talents and skills while you think about your behaviour.

Your behaviour needs to match your goals and your sense of purpose. In order for you to be part of a high performing team or to be the leader of it, your behaviour must be congruent with that goal. For example, there is no point in requiring others to conform to systems unless you do the same yourself. The best performing managers lead by example and create the excellent habits of good work ethics.

Christine was the Managing Director of a high street retailing chain. She was impulsive, creative and highly flexible in what she did. One day she had an inspiration about what the business needed to do to create a new impetus in the business that would lead to great PR and better profitability. She called a meeting for the next day at 8am and insisted that her senior team cancel whatever was in their diary in order to attend. The team was not very pleased to have their schedules disrupted but duly did so. At 8am the next day the whole team was in place in the meeting room. Christine was missing. She had always had a hazy concept of time and arrived just before 8 30. Her whole team was fed up, hugely irritated by her and therefore not prepared to listen. However good her plan was, she lost the impetus by her behaviour and she was no longer taken seriously by her team.

The change you may need to make could be to recognize what it is that you are not doing that could be holding you back. This may be something you could learn. For example, many people in meetings cannot use Excel or read a set of accounts properly. This could be because they have suddenly found themselves in a situation where there has been an assumption that you have this skill or knowledge and there was never the right time to admit that you didn't. Take the opportunity now to work out what you are doing to sabotage your progress and form a plan to resolve it. This could be a simply matter of external or on line training. Perhaps you are a smoker and you are seen to be going outside every hour for a cigarette. If you are working in an organization that is anti-smoking, and let's face it, that seems to be most of the world these days, then work out what your habit is costing you financially and in terms of your career.

Decide now to develop and grow the habits that are useful and helpful. Identify the ones that are holding you back and make a plan to change. Look at your team and identify the behavioural black spots that could be addressed and changed.

Logical level of change – Step Three – Capabilities

Capabilities are the talents and the skills that seem to come to you effortlessly. They are prized assets and go way beyond just academic qualifications or certificates that are objective evidence of what you can do.

Skills and techniques are all things that you can learn. Everything is possible if it is put in the right context. If you want to do something else and learn more skills, work out how you can do it and work out how you can help the others in the organization. A business will thrive and grow if the people in it are increasing their skills and have the will to take on greater challenges.

The next logical level is Beliefs and Values, so in order to set yourself and others down this path to improvement, it can only be done if you believe that you can do it and if it matters to you.

I met Sharon who was a successful accountant who had risen to become Finance Director. She was good at her job and was recognized for her efficiency. She was made redundant at a time when it seemed as though half the accountants in the world were job seeking. After eight months of fruitless job seeking and interviews, Sharon took stock of her situation. Her funds were getting depleted and she realized that the whole situation was affecting her confidence and her belief that she would ever work again. She decided to rent out her house and move to the South of France. She bought a small place there and found a role with an up and coming vineyard. Initially she cooked sophisticated meals for visitors to the vineyard but later learnt more and more about wine making itself. She focused all of her energies on this, invested in the vineyard and used the skills from her past career to make sure that she was creating a business of value. She discovered that by taking control of her own career and adding new knowledge to her existing skill-set, she was happier and more successful

Career opportunities may be closed to you if you lack essential skills for your particular environment. An experienced Human Resources person had his career constantly blocked because he was not qualified to CIPD level. Although he was excellent at his job he could never get to the next level as he lacked credibility.

Look at yourself and your team and define a plan for the next 12 months and implement it. You will be valued because you are recognizing that evolving businesses require evolving people.

Logical level of change – Step Four – Beliefs and Values

Beliefs and values are what drive you in life. These are the fundamental principles that guide your actions. Now is the time to ask yourself if you know what really matters to you in your life and if you are living your life that way. Looking at the next step, Identity, it will be influenced by this sense of knowing who you are.

As a team manager and leader, you will be more effective and more valued by others if you are also considering what is driving the actions of your colleagues.

I interviewed Tony who was a committed Christian and lived a simple life. He did not value possessions or wealth and was more concerned about global poverty and the problems of the developing world. He was the Financial Controller of a PLC and his entire working day revolved around profit, loss, dividends, margins and driving profitable growth. He was unhappy and could not understand why as he was good at his job. He saw an advertisement for a role as Finance Director of an international charity at a much reduced salary and he leapt at the chance. He did not care about the financial impact of the decision as his working life was now flooded with a sense of alignment and purpose.

Logical level of change – Step Five – Identity

This is the chance to find out who you really are and what makes you unique and special. This is not what other people think you are or what labels they may attach to you. This is about the kind of person that you are. It is about what you think about yourself and how other people think of you. Are these things in alignment? Do people see you in the way you want to be seen or is something missing? Self-awareness is the start to personal change and it is only with a heightened sense of who you are that you can move on to think about changing the behaviour of people around you. This thinking about your identity is linked to the final logical level, that of Purpose, your *raison d'etre*, your purpose and your mission.

The best manager is the one who constructs a team around them that will be diverse, adding skills, knowledge and behaviour that mean they have a broad perspective and greater capabilities than others. The key to creating that team is knowing what you are lacking and what you need to be more effective. Self-knowledge means that you can begin to change some of the things about yourself that are holding you back. Some things will never change so this is the chance to draw people into your circle who will compensate for that drawback.

I knew an entrepreneur, John, who was very successful in key elements of his role. He had sound commercial acumen and he knew how to create a business environment that would allow people to play to their strengths. He ran a profitable business but was constantly disappointed by a steady stream of key individuals who resigned and left the business. He knew that he rewarded his people well and could not understand why they were leaving. One night he was away on business with his new Sales Director and they talked until late in the night. The Sales Director told him that no one felt valued by him. John was thought to be too clinical, not interested in people and not willing to share his feelings on what was happening in the business. He was seen to be remote and distant. This was a huge shock to John who did not see that this 'emotional stuff' was important. He decided to use his PA as a trusted sounding board of the feelings in the business and instigated new monthly meetings in an informal setting. He resolved to take steps to get closer to his team and to think about what was important to them rather than what was important to him. The morale of the business changed for the better and he began to gain more than he expected as people started to feel more empowered to give their ideas and opinions.

Logical level of change – Step Six – Purpose

This is the highest level and is the most powerful one that affects all of the other logical levels. This is about questioning your own purpose, ethics and the meaning of your life. This is how you see yourself in relation to the bigger picture of the world. These are the big questions about why you are here and what will your legacy be to the world? Applying this to your organization and your time with a business, think what you want to be remembered for. One of the great ways of having a lasting legacy is being an inspirational role model to others around you.

A clear sense of purpose brings with it a passion and a business's passion is the energy that drives it forward. If you are not passionate about what you and your business are doing, things will always feel a little flat.

At this level it is good to be aware of your place in the grand scheme of things and to know that you are part of a bigger corporate picture. Knowing this will give you the assurance that you have a contribution to make. You will see the bigger picture and you will look around you at your colleagues and seek the same from them. This will fire the corporate and the personal ambition to help you get what you want from your career.

Do you like similarity or difference? – a Metaprogramme

People approach relationships with others in different ways. Some are looking for similarity and some are seeking the difference. This affects how they view change and how they start to think about anything new that is out in front of them

In looking at people, there are different perspectives and we each lean more towards one than the rest:

1. **Similar** – looking for people who are like yourself. Valuing similarity and actively seeking it out and probably excluding those who are not the same out of your circle.
2. **Similar with difference** – preferring people who are similar but tolerant of difference and probably quite interested in it.
3. **Difference** – opposites attract and you like to see how other people think and behave. This fascinates you rather than alarms you.

4. **Difference with similarity** – you like to see variety and difference in the team around you but you quite like to have people with whom you have something in common.

A company was doing very well but kept hitting the same difficulties in their business. They attacked problems with gusto, verve and fast paced action. However, they found they were making costly mistakes as well as making stunning business wins. They wanted to know how they could avoid the mistakes while keeping the success. An analysis of the business quickly showed that it was made up of people who were all the same. Enthusiasm, energy, fast pace and 'Let's go and do it' ruled the business and they recruited in this mode. They came to realize that this meant that they were excluding introverted thinkers from the team so no one was there to pull them back from their action orientation and get them to consider potential pitfalls. They redressed the balance of people in future recruitment activities, looking for people who were different, and the business is still as high octane as ever but making less errors.

The best team is the most diverse, with each team member playing to their strengths. Familiarity often breeds contempt and the biggest danger someone can run in an organization is that others may make assumptions about what they are capable of and for this to be restrictive. Effective people know how to be more than what they are recognized for. Value yourself and your skills, knowing you can do something that is different and challenging is the first step towards gaining that recognition from others.

Clare Howard of Academy 28 says:

'Learn to appreciate people for the achievements they value in themselves and not what you value about yourself; this means you have to pay attention to what makes people tick.'

The team

In order to fit well into a team, start by working through what is important to you and know what you are good at. Ask yourself some searching questions.

Aren't you more than that?

Do you think that what you bring to the team is as much as you can offer or have you other talents and personal attributes you could be contributing? The following exercise is one that will open your mind to the realization that whatever it is you are doing, you can be more than that.

Sit down with someone and in turn ask each other the question 'What are you?' When the person replies, the response should be 'Aren't you more than that?' Respond to that question with a simple 'Yes' and keep going until you run out of time.

Do you now see that this simple exercise is one that has already opened up to you the realization that you have mountains of unexplored potential that you can add to the team?

Now look at your role in the team and consider what you are known for. Put yourself in the position of your colleagues and write the list of what you contribute as they would write it. Do this by visualizing a chair that you usually sit on in meetings and see the places where the others sit. Move from your seat to that occupied by your colleagues and look at yourself through their eyes. What do you see?

1.
2.
3.
4.
5.
6.
7.
8.
9.

The Belbin Model

One of the most recognized models of how a team is constructed is the Belbin Model. It is easy to assimilate and provides definitions of the various roles that team members can contribute and how individuals tend to behave in a team environment.

Meredith Belbin defined the various roles in a team as follows:

Plant: Plants are creative, unorthodox and a generator of ideas and will be bright and free-thinking. Plants can tend to ignore incidentals and refrain from getting bogged down in detail.

Resource Investigator: The Resource Investigator gives a team a rush of enthusiasm at the start of the project by vigorously pursuing contacts and opportunities.

Coordinator: A Coordinator often becomes the default chairperson of a team, stepping back to see the big picture. Coordinators are confident, stable and mature and are very good at delegating tasks to the right person for the job. They clarify decisions, helping everyone else focus on their tasks.

Shaper: The Shaper is a task-focused leader who abounds in nervous energy and with a high motivation to achieve. They are committed to achieving ends and will challenge all comers to achieve objectives.

Monitor Evaluator: Monitor Evaluators are fair and logical observers who assess what is going on. They are often the ones to see all available options with the greatest clarity. They like analytical thought processes and like to work methodically to get to the right decision.

Teamworker: A Teamworker helps to keep the team running. They are good listeners and diplomats, talented at smoothing over conflicts and helping teams work together without conflict.

Implementer: The Implementer is the person who turns other team members' ideas and projects into positive action. They get on with things and like to deliver on time.

Completer Finisher: The Completer Finisher is a perfectionist and likes to see things through to the end. They focus on the detail of projects and are keen on accuracy.

Specialist: Specialists are passionate about learning in their own particular field. As a result, they will have the greatest depth of knowledge, and enjoy imparting it to others. They are constantly improving their wisdom.

Reproduced with kind permission of Belbin
Associates (www.belbin.com).

Whilst models like this are useful and thought provoking and are great for encouraging discussions about the strengths of a team as well as its blind spots, the danger of accepting that you are this person means you can get 'stuck'. Organizations thrive on energy and changing dynamics so be careful not to fall into the trap of thinking that you are a 'Shaper' or a 'Resource Investigator'. Resist the temptation to accept labels that are put upon you. Remember, you are much more than that.

How do you move beyond that definition and ensure that it does not become the fixed perspective that people have of you? How do you show that you have other skills to become the team player who plugs any gaps in the team and covers the blind spots?

Being in a team meeting

Think back to the last time that you were in a meeting. It could be a management meeting, a team briefing or a diverse group brought together for a purpose. It could be the PTA, the local cricket club or the Sports committee of your company. A team is a group of people brought together to achieve a common purpose.

Remember the meeting and think what transpired. How effective was it? Was it fast paced? Was it relevant? Did it stick to the agenda? Did it get diverted? Did it achieve the best possible outcome?

Now look at the personal dynamics around the table. Did everyone make the same kind of contribution with the discussion time divided equally amongst all members or did one or two people dominate the conversation? Inevitably the spread will be uneven with some saying more than others. This is not necessarily because they have more relevant things to say than others. It could be just that they are more assertive, more vocal, and more confident. This is not the same as competence. Looking at contributions in the meeting and assessing it on a scale of 1 to 10, where do you sit? Consider a score of 10 to be when you know you have made a great contribution, leaving the meeting room having said what you think and what you know, putting it across in the most acceptable manner. Not only that, your contribution will also be that you have made sure that other people's voices and opinions have been heard. A score of 1 is when you leave the meeting completely frustrated as your voice has not been heard and you know that the group has missed crucial points that you were aware of and could have volunteered if you had been given the opportunity.

Gareth James of People Plus says:

'Collaboration and cooperation should always be the norm – if others don't want to play, compromise – if they won't compromise, walk away – there's always a loser in a fight and it might be you.'

A typical meeting of any team will include extraverts and introverts. The extraverted style is

SPEAK > THINK > SPEAK

Whereas the introverted style is

THINK > SPEAK > THINK

The consequence of this is that there is a danger in any organization that the introvert's voice is not heard or not heard often enough.

In order for your own performance to improve, you need the team around you to step up their game. How better to achieve this than by supporting and encouraging them? Live by the principle of whole hearted giving and a climate of generosity is bound to emerge.

Matthew Alsop of FCSPD Support says:

'Get involved when opportunities arise like:

♦ Be the one to volunteer to take minutes of meetings. It is a tedious job but somebody has to do it and if you do it, you will be reflecting your perceptions of the meetings. Get control and you will also be the person who has more exposure at the senior management levels in a business.

- ◆ Be part of new initiatives. Taking an active role in key company items will show your willingness to help and support the organization.
- ◆ Does your company support a charity or look for volunteers for certain events? Don't sit back, get involved.'

Strategies to help you achieve this in your next meeting

1. Ensure that you aim to be in deep rapport with the person you have identified as being the one who is most reticent and therefore least likely to speak without encouragement.
2. Observe closely and carefully. Remember eye movements? Watch for the tell-tale signs about how this person is recollecting data and situations.
3. Actively win their contribution to the meeting by saying something:
   'I am wondering if George has something to add to this topic?' or
   'I know that Mary has first hand knowledge of this so would you let us know what you think?'
4. Pause.
5. Prevent others from filling the silence.
6. If forced, introduce a tangible way of preventing interruptions, such as the golden pen – only the person with golden pen may speak.

The powerful position of collecting and encouraging the contributions of all team members will be one that makes you stand out. No one likes a selfish person so be renowned for your generosity and your skills in getting the best out of everyone. This will reflect on all and you will be seen as someone who is capable of extracting maximum value from the team.

Gareth James of People Plus says:

'Only play politics if you are a master politician; amateurs derail quickly.'

Managing your relationship with your boss

Your path from good to great will be smoothed if you have a clear relationship with your boss where you have excellent rapport and you communicate well. The relationship need not always be harmonious but you always need to be seen to be part of the team. What do you do if things are going slightly off track and how do you identify the tell-tale signs that all is not as well as it could be? Look out for changes in rapport that could be seen in a number of ways:

♦ **Eye contact** Is your boss avoiding your eyes? If you have worked there long enough, you will know what level of eye contact is normal. If this suddenly starts to change, then notice it, ask yourself 'What is the meaning of this?' Perhaps it is nothing to do with you and your behaviour. It might be that they have problems of their own and they do not want to share them with you. It could also be that they are avoiding giving some news to you that could be anywhere on the scale of insignificant to major impact.

♦ **Solution?** Decide to find a way to win their confidence and find out what is going on. This way you will win in two ways, firstly by giving them the relief of disclosure and secondly you will win as you know what is going on. Hard facts are never as scary as feared facts.

♦ **Face time** Perhaps you are suddenly finding that the amount of time you are spending with your boss is diminishing. You might not notice at first but suddenly you begin to see a pattern developing. Your boss seems to be avoiding being alone with you and is cancelling meetings.

♦ **Solution?** Make your goal to increase your time with your boss. Ensure that your will to achieve this goal is greater than theirs to avoid you. The focus of your decision is to move towards something, that is to say, increased time with the boss, whereas their goal is one of avoidance. A clearly formed, positive goal will always win the day. Then use this time to establish deep rapport and get to the bottom of the issue.

♦ **Language** Be ready for nuances in tone in all communications, that is the tone in meetings as well as telephone conversations and e-mails.

♦ **Feedback** You are no longer included in important projects. As with Sign No. 2, it's essential to look at this from a relative point of view. If your department isn't getting any essential projects, the department is the problem, and you'd best be looking to get out of there and go where the action is. However, if key projects are still coming in, but they are going to your peers, it's not a good sign.

♦ **A negative tone** Responses to your ideas take on a need-lessly negative tone, with phrases such as, 'You need to understand that I'm trying to run a business here', which implies that somehow you are oblivious to the fact that you work for a business.

Even the toughest of bosses may shy away from direct feed-back, so don't assume that you're getting on well. If it's been a while since you've had a performance discussion with your boss, ask for one. This is not a guarantee that you'll get back in good standing. It will provide you with an opportunity to show your skills to turn situations round and to use the team to deliver better results. Show your willingness to take tough feedback and to use that feedback to show a new perspective.

Remember: the world is a friendly place and people you are working with generally want to do well and to cooperate. Tap into this to build an active and a powerful team.

Networking

HOW TO GET MORE PEOPLE IN YOUR LIFE AND ADD ZEST TO YOUR GOALS

"People are not their behaviours; accept the person and change the behaviour"

NLP encourages people to get to know other great people. Surround yourself with people who are like you and who share your values. That's essential. Include in your circle people who you admire, who have achieved the kind of success that you would like to have and suddenly you are working with a new kind of energy. Think about when you are surrounded by people who are not like you. It can be a draining experience as you have to fight the feelings of jarring against them. If you are a naturally positive person, think how tricky it is to be with those who have a negative slant. Those who moan, complain and see the worst in everything are people who feast on the energy of others. Break away and stay away. There is an NLP saying: 'People are only doing the best they can with the resources they have available.' It stands to reason, therefore, that the more resources you have, the more successful you will be – and the best resources are human. It is now time to upgrade your human resources and inject new energies into your circle.

Leave the wrong ones behind

Before we look at expanding your network and forging contacts with successful people, take this opportunity to look at your existing network and your social circle. Imagine you are in a concert hall and you have a front seat in the stalls, looking at an empty stage. Play some music that you like so it is playing around you and you feel comfortable in this empty theatre. Look at the stage and begin to invite people to appear on it. These can be school friends, work colleagues, university friends, family, acquaintances, customers, neighbours, friends from clubs, the pub or teams. Invite them on one by one and look at them carefully as they face you in the safe environment where you see them but they cannot see you.

Now look at them individually and ask yourself if their friendship is true and if it is real. Consider if what you experience together is something that is positive, friendly, creative and mutually useful. If it has become a relationship of habit that destroys more than it creates, invite that person to leave the stage. Do this for each one and then see who is left in the inner sanctum of friendship. Notice also just how many gaps there are and decide now how you plan to fill them with people who are relevant to your place in life as it is today.

Who do you know?

People used to be valued for their 'little black book', probably now replaced by the number of contacts they have on www. linkedin.com or contacts in Microsoft Outlook. People with the best books were the ones with a window on the world, the capability to tap into other resources and bring new insights and different perspectives to the table. How many times have I written in interview comments that a particular candidate has an up to date and relevant list of contacts? This is pertinent not just for sales people but for engineers, technical people and innovators across the board, anyone who is working in today's technology driven society where the rate of pace is frantic and people who slip behind are left behind.

Unless you are a recluse, doing something that requires no interaction whatsoever with people, you need to improve the way you forge links with colleagues, customers, competitors and industry leaders. This will add value for you and it will add value for them. Because you want to go from good to great, you will realize that you need to be tapping into a greater resource of people than you are doing at the moment. However good your network is, it could be better. No matter how many connections you have on www.linkedin.com or Facebook, you could have more and you could link with people who are more relevant to your current stage in life and business.

For your contribution as a networker therefore, let's establish a goal. Whatever your network looks like at the moment, decide now to reinforce your relationships with the people you already know and that you will increase your connections by a certain number a month. How many? Who?

Options will include:

♦ Colleagues. These could be in your office, another office, a different location. If you work for a global company, who do you know in different regions?
♦ Suppliers. It could be the person who delivers your stationery, the sandwich delivery person or someone who supplies the bulk of your raw material.
♦ Customers. Is your contact base sufficiently broad? Do you do enough things for them? Engaging with them is what will give you deep roots and allow you increased access to their plans and what you can do for them.
♦ Total strangers who currently have no line in to your life and who do not yet know that they have a role to play. These could be people you meet at an exhibition, a seminar, a conference or a client lunch that you are secretly planning to miss. How will you ever know?

Clare Howard of Academy 28 says:

'Keep in touch. Have a network inside and outside the company and treat it like a vegetable garden i.e. sow, transplant, take cuttings from other people, water it, feed it, and know when it's time to prune and cut out the deadwood and the drift wood.'

The most important network is the internal network

If you have just joined an organization, then you need to know who is who and they need to know who you are. Quietly getting on and doing a good job is not enough. You have to be seen to be doing a good job. By having knowledge of who is who in the business you will be able to help them and they will be able to help you. The great people in the business are those with a diverse and strong up to date internal network. Picture how useful this will be when decisions are being made about redundancies, promotions, transfers and salary increases. If people don't know who you are, you will never be on the list.

Anchors

In the world of NLP, an anchor is a stimulus that evokes a consistent response. This is the simplicity of cause and effect. If one thing happens, such as hearing a noise, seeing a sight, or feeling an emotion, then exactly the same reaction happens every time. For example, if you see a red traffic light, you stop. If you hear a piece of music that was played at a significant event, you will instantly be transported back there in your mind. These can work well for you and in some cases are vital for survival but others are not so useful. Anchors are very relevant to networking but while you are thinking about them in this chapter, please reflect on their value and importance in so many other areas. Looking at the other eight attributes that we have already covered, a positive anchor to help reinforce your positive attitude, your confidence, your energy and your curiosity would inject that certainty to help you get there. Not only that, a positive anchor to help in communication and decision making as well as helping you remember to be a flexible team worker would be the secret weapon that will see you through.

Powerful people in business are aware of what triggers unhelpful emotions and responses and they work to create anchors that put them in Peak State. This is the state that refers to when someone is performing or feeling at their best. What is Peak State for one person is not necessarily what will be the same for another. Imagine a business where you have everyone working in that state of heightened senses where they are giving their best. Start by working out what are the resources for Peak State for you and then move on to your team. This is something that is under your control and will give you a team of high performing people.

Positive Anchors

Positive Anchors are those triggers that happen at an unconscious level that make you surer of yourself, happier, positive, receptive and able to achieve more, powered by recollections of previous events that were successful and happy for you.

How can you use them to help you with people and growing a network? The most obvious anchor of a meeting is a business card. We have this ritual of exchanging cards to facilitate further contact so develop this positive anchor one stage further to create a better impression.

My personal favourite is to send a hand written note or a card to someone to thank them for hospitality or help they may have given me. An e-mail or a text does not stand out as they flood into your inbox with so many others. Why not decide to be noticed? A card will appear on someone's desk and probably will stay there for a while, a permanent reminder of who you are.

Tim Smits is the renowned former record producer who moved to Cornwall, unearthed the lost gardens of Heligan, and then founded the Eden Project. He is famed for his idiosyncratic yet extraordinarily successful way of growing business. He addressed the Institute of Directors conference in the Royal Albert Hall in 2009 and he emphasized the power that meeting people has had and continues to have on his life. He said that you don't know who you are meant to know so you have to put yourself in a position where you stand a chance of meeting them. He accepts every seventh invitation he receives, regardless of where it comes from so that he invites the unknown and the unexpected into his world.

You could also use the resources that you have already to bring pleasure to people. If you have photos that were taken at a lunch or a PR launch event, take the photos and send them to people who will be interested. You could do this electronically at no cost or you could push the boat out and get them printed off for a trifling sum. Business is not only about the objective and the impersonal. It is also about recognizing the individual and ensuring that they know that you are treating them like this. Create a portfolio of anchors that will ensure you are always front of mind. You could be the person who brings in cakes on Fridays or who puts a bunch of flowers in the meeting room. These are low cost and high impact. You are actively creating links between who you are and how people instinctively think of you.

Etta Cohen, Managing Director, Forward Ladies www.forwardladies. com

Etta Cohen agreed to have lunch with a female business friend and the time they spent together was so constructive that they agreed to meet again the next month and each would bring a friend. The formula worked and the network grew rapidly. The simple formula was that it was informal, friendly and free with the sole objective of connecting with business women on a regular basis. Businesses in the region were quick to recognize the power of this newly formed group and were queuing up to offer their services that included training workshops, lunches, speakers, events in every imaginable venue. The events include formal gatherings, presentations, learning programmes and some are just plain fun. Delegations of Yorkshire Women, now under the banner of Forward Ladies, travelled to Paris, Hong Kong, Barcelona, Latvia and Italy. Five years on with a network that now has 3500+ members and a website that attracts over 5000 hits per month, Etta still keeps things simple and still encourages networking skills in others. She leads by example and the values of the organization are that it is good to give because it is this reciprocity that delivers business results. Millions of pounds of business have been generated through connections made because of Forward Ladies and Etta is now driving its growth nationally and internationally. She says, 'If you have a strong network that you actively manage, you will be better regarded, more powerful and more useful. Business is about networking, managing contacts and who you know.'

Make it a priority now to create a new positive anchor in your team. You could decide that everyone has to send an e mail at 5pm on Friday setting out the successes of the week. You could designate one day a month as a non-internal e-mail day. Whatever you do, make it your choice to offer a resource to your team that will be for the benefit of all.

Negative anchors

Negative anchors can be draining and evoke the kind of response that you don't want, such as fear, sadness, guilt or anger. This is not a useful resource state to have so part of success is avoiding those negative anchors that trigger such a state. Recognizing what they are and being ready to get out of their way is a handy skill to have. The alternative is to allow yourself to be overpowered by feelings you are helpless to stop. People who are great in the workplace are in control and know what they are doing.

I worked with a Marketing Director of an advertising agency in London. She was well regarded by all. She found herself unable to deal with any form of conflict as it reminded her of unhappy arguments in her home when she was growing up. Her response to situations of apparent dispute and heated debate was for her eyes to well with tears and to begin to cry. Her colleagues felt uncomfortable and secretly despised her for her apparent weakness.

Recognizing that she needed to address this, she decided to access a more useful state when faced with an argument. She replaced the memories of family rows with an image of a successful business outcome after vigorous debate and thus was able to control her emotions.

Another perspective on this is being aware of what brings out negative responses in others. These are not necessarily rational so be prepared for anything. I have a client who is enraged by the sight of people with takeaway coffees. All he has to do is to see a Starbucks cup and the same diatribe ensues, with dark mutterings about the coffee being carried as though it is 'their mother's ashes.' This is not a useful state for him and the consequence for people working with him is that they have to distract him and get him back on track. Simply by appearing in front of him with a coffee in a mug would resolve all of that. You are not there to change the world, just to accommodate yourself to elements of it that are not worth fighting over.

Take the opportunity to think of things that are triggers for you to respond in an unhelpful way. This could be the communal kitchen being left in a mess, the same person arriving late for a meeting, the squeaking of a pen on a white board or the persistent clicking of a pen off and on. My personal negative anchor is the iPod listeners who have the volume turned up so loud that people around can hear the tinny beat.

The emotions that this kind of event can arouse are not helpful. People will see you are rattled and will take note. In the same way, you will see the triggers of others.

Getting rid of your own negative anchors

First of all, work out what they are. Identify them in order to eradicate. As long as they are in your life, you will be at their mercy so it is time to get back in control and work to get rid of them once and for all. These are acting at an unconscious level so by thinking about them now, you are taking the first step to excising them from your life.

1.
2.
3.
4.
5.

A new chain of anchors

One trigger for behaviour and a response usually sets off another. Working out what the trigger is will allow you to build up a chain of anchors that will consist of different small steps that allow you to break the pattern of response and create a new one. It is too much to hope that you can move instantly from a state of irritation to one of calmness. The route to calmness is one that has milestones along the way. For example, to remove the irritation of iPods, one step could be to inject humour. Imagine a large pair of scissors cutting through the headphones so that the listener is now sent into bewildering world of silence. Or you could integrate the tinny noise into a tune on your head, gradually turning up your own noise until it disappears and is drowned out. The final stage could be that this is a positive anchor for you to bring out your own iPod and find the time to listen to something that you enjoy.

Growing your network

If you are one of those people who feels slightly reticent about expanding your network, feeling slightly held back by something or if you are simply looking to improve, let's look at a number of techniques that could help develop essential skills. What might be preventing you from getting to know the people you don't know who will play a part in your life? You have now looked at possible limiting beliefs in Chapter 5 so consider what you might be thinking about yourself or others that could be holding you back. Think about them and take the time now to be honest with yourself to accept them and then be strict with yourself to impose the discipline to get rid of them.

If you have had unfortunate experiences in the past with networking, now is the time to use the reframing techniques that we discussed in Chapter 5. Perhaps you remember going to events and sitting on the sidelines, nursing a warm glass of wine or water, conscious that everyone else seemed to know people. A possible reframe of this is that now you are in a different place in your life. Previously you believed the universe to be slightly intimidating and threatening. You are now someone who has a purpose to your networking and this will give you the confidence to approach anyone you see. You have also developed a number of 'small talk' introductions to help you through. Networking now has a more useful context so you can do it.

External connections

However powerful or well connected you may be inside the place where you work, great people have external connections. They may not necessarily be work related and they may be casual rather than scheduled. These are the places you go to test your skills, explore new ideas and meet people who provide you with the advice, help and the reassurance you need to grow and develop. This group of people with different outlooks and different dynamics are the ones who can flag up different ways of doing things.

Alex Mitchell, Head of Influencer Relations at the Institute of Directors, believes that networking is not a dark art. By helping and supporting people you meet along the way, he believes that you create a sense of trust. An open and honest exchange ensures that supply chains are robust. This engagement with others draws customers into feeling part of your brand so networking becomes a crucial part of how you set out the passion of how your business performs. Networking is not something flimsy and superficial. It is a way to demonstrate integrity and build relationships that last.

The path of social media

The Internet causes us to be plugged into the universe. If you are not plugged in, you are shut out. Modern business has no place for technophobes. Embrace new technologies and use what they have to offer to help you develop a presence and to grow the brand that is you.

As well as www.linkedin.com you will want to explore the value of Facebook. Worked at properly it will give you the chance to find people you know, people you have forgotten about and people you have yet to meet. For many people Facebook is a positive anchor that indicates you are networked and modern. When you use it, always be aware of the potential pitfalls of loose language that projects an image you would rather not have. See it as a public platform for development and control the messages that you send.

The vogue that is Twitter

Although the jury is still out on the business benefit of Twitter, it is worth considering how you could use it to help you. If you decide that you are going to have a Twitter presence, the initial challenge is that 140 characters are not a lot. You have one long sentence to transmit a message that will be seen by others and will convey an impression of who you are and how you think.

Strategy for Twitter

Start with the end in sight. How do you wish to be seen? Why are you doing it? If it is just for fun and for your friends, then be sure to protect your updates unless you want your boss, your colleagues and your potential future bosses to have access to your thoughts. Google has a long memory that can be personally damaging. If you tweet in order to gain and to give knowledge, if it is to create a brand awareness for your company and for yourself, then be clear now about your goal. For what purpose are you on Twitter?

Then look at the profile which provides an opportunity for you to give a brief overview of who you are. Choose your words carefully as you don't have many and you have no control over who might be reading them. Decide how you wish to be perceived by others and always put things in a positive light. You will be looking at high level, big chunk words that position you where you want to be and how you want to be seen. What you think you are writing is not necessarily what people will be reading. The meaning of the communication is the response you receive.

One of my candidates told me the story of Jane. She was out in her car and she crashed it. Once she got over the shock, she sent out a plaintive tweet to her friends and connections in the Twitter world. A sympathetic friend responded instantly ending her message LOL. The meaning for her was 'lots of love'. The meaning received was 'laugh out loud'. An unseemly public exchange of cross words then ensued.

However much one may love technology and the benefits that it brings to business today and however much one might be thrilled by the networking opportunities that it brings with it, always remember that it is only one route of many.

Face time

Are you in danger of relying too much on technology to deliver the message you want to send? Great people find time for meetings and the invaluable information that comes from the unexpected. E-mails and telephone conversations are dangerous as they can become transactional. You need to convey a message and you deliver it. The person responds and the job is done. What you will probably never find out is what other concerns your colleague or customers might have. You may miss valuable opportunities to do business, create projects, initiate change or new ideas as you have not created the space around you for it to surface.

One of my clients had a Sales Director called David who one day was asked by a customer to drive to their offices for a discussion about an ongoing project. David was annoyed as he had planned to send through his thoughts and proposals by e-mail. He now had an hour's drive ahead of him, an hour for the meeting and then the return trip. All he could focus on was the loss of half his working day.

He went along to the meeting and discovered that the customer's boss was in the meeting too and then what was supposed to be an hour's meeting stretched into an invitation to join them for lunch. He was then part of a freewheeling debate about the customer's plans and he had the chance to make suggestions that would benefit both the customer and David's business. He left the meeting with ideas about what else he could do to create value in his organization and within a week had put a proposal to the customer that was met with approval. Not only this but he now also had a higher level contact in an important client and he had taken steps to prove his worth. He realized that an e-mail delivery of his work would have demonstrated his competence and his timeliness. His involvement in a face to face meeting gave him the chance to become a trusted insider as well.

What might you be missing?

Sometimes you see what you expect to see and you miss things that are right in front of you. It is time to take steps to adjust your vision and increase the scope of what you notice. When you are embarking on a project, have you made sure that you have taken notice of the views and knowledge of people closest to you? Sometimes hours of time can be saved by engaging with people around you. The internal company network can bring you insights because of their company knowledge and experience.

When you are busy looking for someone new to join the company, have you checked the talent in all areas of your own organization? I have known countless companies suddenly discover that they have people with talent and potential who are doing temping jobs or working as warehouse operatives. Are you sure you know who all your people are and what they are capable of?

When you are grabbing a coffee in the office kitchen, instead of chatting about what was on TV last night or the state of the weather, talk to someone you scarcely know and find out more about them. Their skills will become open to you and their network will be too – but only if you take the time to find out.

The more you notice, the more you can bring into your decision-making process. You may see more people and be aware of their strengths that could be added value to you and to the business.

Peripheral vision

Try this exercise to stretch your boundaries:

Draw a large black spot about the size of a saucer and place it on a wall in front of you. You can be outside or inside, it doesn't matter. Without focusing on anything in particular, look straight ahead. Look at the black spot and then gradually allow yourself to notice simultaneously what is happening on either side. You are looking straight ahead and you are also seeing what is happening out of the corner of each eye. Keep your focus directly in front of you and increase the scope of what you see by noticing what is happening at either side. Once you have mastered this peripheral vision, keep practicing so that you become adept at seeing more and more. Try doing this when you are sitting in a restaurant so you are aware of what is happening at the tables alongside you. As you become more skilled you will be able to gain an impression of what they are saying and what the atmosphere is like. You are attuned to your environment in a more powerful way and things will not escape you.

Resolving difficult relationships

There are times when, having used all your skills in creating rapport and all of your best language skills, you simply cannot get on with someone. It may not happen often but when it does it can be a major impediment to your growth inside the organization. You may be faced with someone who you do not like. You might find yourself saying:

He is so arrogant
She is so pedantic
He always thinks he's right
He isn't as smart as he thinks he is
She always rubs people up the wrong way
He is so horribly ambitious
She never gets things done

He promises more than he can deliver
She is always late

Consider the thought that when you are recognizing others as being irritating and off putting in some way, you are only able to see it for what it is because you are recognizing part of yourself. Unless it was part of your make up, how would you know what it is? Perception is projection. You are seeing what you are and what you do not value in yourself and you are rejecting these qualities in others as being unacceptable. Just as it is easier to get on well with people who reflect what we value most in ourselves, so it is hard to want to be with people whose recognizable behaviour is what we would like to eradicate from our own personalities.

Other people choose how they behave and we all choose how we want to interpret or perceive their behaviour. Take this to the next step and it means that people in our lives will act the way we unconsciously want them to. We get what we focus on and therefore we project onto others how we want them to act. Once this projection flashes onto our consciousness, it becomes our own projection.

This means that you will see in people whatever you want to see, and you will only perceive things that you have in you.

However unpalatable this may seem to you, the next time you are in a meeting and feel a spark of impatience or irritation or dislike of someone who is speaking, reflect on what exactly it is that is causing this feeling. Then look inside yourself and see where it lies within you.

The impact of this restraint and reflection is that you are less likely to be ready to form fixed views on whether or not you like someone. You won't jump to conclusions and you will be more likely to give someone the benefit of the doubt and look past their apparent faults and seek out the good points.

It is unrealistic to expect to like everyone you have to work with and yet by recognizing that this unfavourable perception that you are holding onto may be a projection of who you are yourself, you will become fairer, more humble and more ready to accept the diversity and similarity of others.

> Remember: engaging with others, connecting with people you don't know yet that you need to know will give the extra resources you need to continue adding value at every level of your career.

Glossary of NLP Terms Used on the Road from Good to Great

Anchor—This is the physical, auditory, kinaesthetic or visual stimulus that triggers a consistent response. It depends on consistent replication of what the anchor is as well as the right kind of timing. You can see anchors, hear them, touch them or find them in specific points in your environment.

Auditory—Sounds you hear, sounds you make and language you prefer.

Cause and effect—People who are 'at cause' accept full responsibility for their actions and the results of their decisions. People who are 'at effect' behave more like victims who blame others for what has happened to them. Life is not under their control.

Chunking down—This is deliberately moving down to specific and concrete levels of detail and information. This is done by breaking down big plans and ideas into smaller pieces.

Chunking up—This is moving up from the specific and the detailed to the more abstract and broader picture, aiming for a bigger plan and perspective.

Eye accessing—This is observing the movement of eyes to indicate how someone is thinking.

Goals—Individual and personal aspirations for clearly defined specific outcomes. What someone wants.

Kinaesthetic—What do you touch and feel?

Logical levels—These are the progressive levels of personal growth that lead to the ultimate goal of understanding your own sense of purpose.

Map of the World—This is the individual's unique interpretation of their own world, constructed from their own experiences and perceptions.

Matching—This is taking parts of other people's body language and behaviour and by copying it, increasing rapport with others.

Mirroring—This is the deliberate matching of someone's body language in order to help create better rapport.

Pacing—This is matching and mirroring certain aspects of someone else's behaviour in order to increase rapport quickly.

Leading—Once rapport has been achieved through successful mirroring and matching, then changing your own behaviour with subtlety in order to encourage others to follow what you are doing and how you are doing it. This is the way to alter the behaviour of others.

Neuro Linguistic Programming—
1. Neuro – the mind – how people think, feel and imagine
2. Linguistic – language – spoken, written, unwritten
3. Programming –the technical side of how to influence the mind through language.

Neuro Linguistic Programming is a constantly growing collection of techniques and tools that allows people to achieve their goals. It is based on careful use of language, modeling excellence and a range of fast and effective interventions.

Presuppositions of NLP—These are the underlying assumptions of NLP that form its core beliefs.

Rapport—This is the way to establish trust, unspoken understanding and cooperation with others in order to build more effective relationships.

Reframing—This is the fast and effective way of deliberately changing the context of events through carefully constructed language to give events or statements another, more constructive meaning.

Representational systems—This is the way that you experience life through your five senses: visual, auditory, kinaesthetic, olfactory and gustatory.

Swish pattern—A way to change unwanted habits or habitual responses that are not useful. The swish pattern produces new and more positive ways of doing things.

Visual—What you see.

About the Author

Anne Watson has spent almost 30 years in the business of high level, headhunting based recruitment. She works with clients internationally, including the UK, Asia, Continental Europe and the Americas. Her clients range from PLCs to small private businesses who all see the need to attract talent into their business and, having done so, then face the challenge of ensuring these people are able to make the best possible contribution. Anne has always been intrigued by people and has wanted to know how to make sure that individuals are placed in the environment that will bring the best out of them. This curiosity has led her to explore many tools to assist them, including more than ten years working with NLP, applying its techniques to career success.

She has coauthored two books with Heather Summers, *The Book of Luck* and *The Book of Happiness*, and her most recent book is *The Definitive Job Book*, a distillation of her experience to help the active job hunter.

After graduating from St Andrews University with an M.A. (Hons) in Hispanic Languages and Literature, she worked in the Immigration Service and spent two years in Pakistan with her husband Martin.

Visit www.annewatson.co.uk to do the enlarged questionnaire and to get more resources to help on your path from good to great.

Acknowledgements

I am sure that this book would never have been completed without the constant smiling trust of my husband Martin and children Tom and Eleanor. I listened in dismay to their utter confidence that I would finish the book on time and I felt I just had to get up a bit earlier and go to bed a bit later in order to do what I said I would do. I would like to thank them whole-heartedly for that and wonder if next time they could just let me off the hook a little bit and set the bar a fraction lower?

This book is the result of the experiences and relationships that I have had over the years with friends, family, clients, candidates and people I have met along the way. The richness of those experiences has ensured that I have been privileged to be part of people's lives, careers, learnings and businesses.

Many people have helped me by contributing their thoughts for this book. Clare Howard's encouragement and reflections were invaluable and she lifted my spirits when everything seemed hopeless. Kate Burton kindly offered NLP expertise when I needed another viewpoint. Business colleagues and friends agreed to be quoted, as you will see, so my thanks go to Gareth James, John Dargan, David Apicella, Etta Cohen, Matthew Alsop and Alex Mitchell. Thank you also to the people who responded to my request for market research – Nathaniel Jacob, Elizabeth Davison, Helen Cogan, Catherine Owen, Hannah Waring and Byron Fitzpatrick. David Powell also showed me a different way to travel.

None of this would have happened though without the wonderful team at Capstone Wiley who gave me the opportunity to write a book about something that is truly inspiring – the path from good to great. This was my chance to set out NLP techniques in an appropriate business environment and I was thrilled to be able to do it. It all happened because of the skills, support, ideas, energy, encouragement and friendship of the whole team, Holly Bennion, Scott Smith, Iain Campbell, Megan Varilly, Grace O'Byrne and Jenny Ng. Capstone – what a team!

Biodata – The People Who Commented along the Way

Matthew Alsop – Managing Director, FCSPD Support

Matthew Alsop is the lead consultant of FCSPD Support (www.fcspdsupport.co.uk). The team helps small and new start-up businesses in Scotland by empowering them through dynamic commercial support.

He began his career working for Rolls-Royce in the North East of England. Always ready to take on a new challenge, he moved abroad and gained outstanding international experience in Austria and India before finally returning and settling in Scotland.

Working in a range of organizations from high tech mass production through to complex heavy engineering, his roles have been equally diverse from Finance Director to senior sales positions.

Success in his career to date has been driven by an innate ability to empathize with others and clearly communicate common goals. His traditional style of management adapts quickly to changing environments and has a strong results focus, making him a unique resource in any business situation.

David Apicella-European Human Resources Director, MeadWestVaco

David Apicella is currently the HR Director for MeadWestVaco, a $6 billion turnover US-owned organization employing over 20 000 people. He has over 15 years' industry experience within significant blue chip organizations and has a wealth of international HR experience in a variety of disciplines. In his newly appointed role he is now predominately focused to deliver organizational effectiveness to the 37 European businesses and specializes in managing change and organizational design. He also continues to maintain overall HR responsibility for the UK, Ireland and Netherlands, covering 11 sites. David has a BA (Hons.) degree in HR Management and is a Member of the Chartered Institute of Personnel and Development and BPS level B qualified.

Etta Cohen – Forward Ladies

Etta Cohen is the founder of Forward Ladies, one of the North's fastest growing women's business networking and support groups. She began her working life as a teacher but a divorce and two young children to support led her to make some dramatic changes.

Taking on the role of mother, father and breadwinner, she began working for Leeds Training Council, a whole new world and a big step from the security of teaching which she had done for 22 years. She then went on to become a business development manager at regional development agency Yorkshire Forward.

The idea of Forward Ladies began in 2000 with a lunch, which proved so successful that Etta suggested a further meeting with each woman inviting a guest. Since then, the organization has grown with the members driving it forward and it now has a database of over 3700 business women.

Forward Ladies provides members with the opportunity to meet like-minded business women in an informal, professional environment and acts as a business support network offering training and mentoring to help women develop themselves and their businesses.

John Dargan – Entrepreneur and Business Leader

John is a strategically focused and operationally effective business driver who has an outstanding track record of success as an inspirational leader of a global business. He has an entrepreneurial ability to create a dynamic business environment where successful teams understand, embrace and realize his vision. Pace, passion, energy and determination to find creative solutions in a commercially successful and customer focused manner are the hallmarks of this technologically innovative Chief Executive whose leadership gives companies their powerful set of values. Through his ability to create a compelling and ambitious vision for organizations, John has an outstanding track record of building global businesses where people believe in themselves and exceed their own expectations.

Clare Howard-Managing Director, Academy 28

Clare is a change and learning consultant with over 20 years' experience working on organizational learning and development projects. Managing Director of Academy 28, she has worked with top organizations across Europe to help them implement strategic plans in areas such as change leadership, coaching and mentoring programmes, leadership skills, self-managed development, and international training programmes to implement new technologies, processes and systems.

Her philosophy is that you can invent your own future, wherever you start from. So her professional life has taken her from researching medieval Florentine entrepreneurs, international traders and spin-doctors (the ultimate in networkers), through to hands on project management, women's grass-roots development projects, as well as large-scale training and organizational initiatives. Clare embraces the opportunities offered by new technologies and mobile communications to help individuals, teams and organizations maximize learning and development. However, therein lies a secret. Her use of all things technological has its origin in enlightened self-interest – because, with the aid of phone and high-speed internet, she can spend as much time as possible living her alternative lifestyle in her house and garden and retreat centre in the south of France.

Gareth James – Director, People Plus Ltd
People Plus was set up by Gareth in 1993 after an 18-year career as a Personnel/HR generalist, his final role being an International HR Director for a sector of the Rhone Poulenc group, covering Africa, Asia, Australasia and Latin America as well as the UK.

Gareth's passion is the development of people and People Plus provides a portfolio of services for clients across the private and public sectors both in the UK and overseas. Gareth's main area of activity is organizational development and change management, career management, executive coaching and team development.

Gareth's personal development has included 12 programmes in psychometrics and assessment, 360° Feedback, Transactional Analysis and NLP.

When Gareth is not working he will be found either inside a theatre, opera house or concert hall or travelling to exotic places (100 countries visited and he's not finished yet!)

Alex Mitchell-Head of Influencer Relations, Institute of Directors

Alex started off his career at the Confederation of British Industry (CBI) until he moved to the Institute of Directors (IoD) in 2005, where he is currently the Head of Influencer Relations. During his time at the IoD, Alex has held a number of roles, which entails close liaison with IoD members and the wider business community on subjects ranging from leadership, entrepreneurialism and employment to innovation, technology and global markets. In his current role he has developed close relationships with the government, opposition parties and key trade organizations, working with them to enhance the competitiveness of UK businesses at home and abroad.

Alex attended Llandovery College and then went on to study Marine Biology and Environmental Science at the University of Portsmouth, where he graduated with honours in 2000. He is a keen cyclist and fencer, and is a governor of a secondary school in Lambeth, London.

Other Books that You May Find Useful

Belbin, Meredith R. *Team Roles At Work*, Butterworth-Heinemann 1996

Burton, Kate and Platts, Brinley *Building Confidence For Dummies*, John Wiley & Sons 2006

Charvet, Shelle Rose, *Words That Change Minds*, Kendall/Hunt 1995

Egan, Gerard, *Working The Shadow Side*, Jossey Bass 1994

Knight, Sue, *NLP At Work*, Nicholas Brealey 1995

Molden, David, *Managing With the Power of NLP*, Prentice Hall 1996

Molden, David, *NLP Business Masterclass*, Prentice Hall 2001

O'Neil, John R. *The Paradox of Success*, McGraw-Hill 1995

Ready, Romilla and Burton, Kate, *Neuro-Linguistic Programming For Dummies*, John Wiley & Sons 2004

Ready, Romilla and Burton, Kate, *Neuro-Linguistic Programming Workbook For Dummies*, John Wiley & Sons 2008

Other books by Anne Watson

Summers, Heather and Watson, Anne, *The Book of Luck*, Capstone 2004

Summers, Heather and Watson, Anne, *The Book of Happiness*, Capstone 2006

Watson, Anne, *The Definitive Job Book*, Capstone 2007

Index